T0160701

THE MILLIONAIRE JOSHUA

THE
MILLIONAIRE
JOSHUA

HIS PROSPERITY SECRETS FOR YOU!

Catherine Ponder

DeVorss Publications
Camarillo, California

The Millionaire Joshua
Copyright © 1978 by Catherine Ponder

ISBN: 9780875162539
Library of Congress Control Number: 77-086719

DeVorss & Company, Publisher
P.O. Box 1389
Camarillo CA 93011-1389
www.devorss.com

Printed in the United States of America

CONTENTS

The Author's Invitation to You!

How the millionaires of the Bible can help you. How the millionares of the Bible have prospered the author. What Joshua's success can mean to you. What Joshua's success has meant to the author. A prosperity invitation to you.

Joshua's life—Part I—as a slave in Egypt. Joshua's prosperous background. Joshua's prosperity was linked to that of Jesus. The Egyptian's secret name for success was passed on to the Hebrews. Joshua's song of success. How you can use this "song of success." Joshua's awareness of the prosperity laws. Joshua's life—Part II—in the wilderness. Moses was Joshua's prosperity teacher. Why the Promised Land of Canaan symbolized unlimited wealth. How a housewife prospered herself and others. The significance of Joshua acting as Moses' servant. How Joshua's love of the law helped the author. Joshua's life—Part III—in the Promised Land. Joshua as the prosperous saviour of the Hebrews. Joshua's success as a tribal hero and military leader. Joshua as a business executive and statesman. The closing prosperity secrets of Joshua.

Why the abundance report of the two prosperous-minded spies was rejected. What happens if you do not mentally accept your good? The prosperity law of mental acceptance works through two steps. Can you release limitation? How release of a $5,000 loss brought $2,500 and an inheritance. How release brought much-needed second car plus peace of mind and family happiness. How forming a vacuum brought pets, furnishings and a new job. How to take only the good from each experience and let the rest go. How release brought a better job and payment of old debts. Release brings new job, home and boyfriend for the daughter. It brings healing and trip abroad for the mother. How release brings freedom for daughter from undesirable relationship. How forgiveness and release brought healings and money. How to start thinking about your life the way you want it to be. How a poor boy got an education and prospered. How Joshua turned delay into a blessing. The rich rewards and how to claim them.

How the Law of Attraction works. How Joshua used the Law of Attraction to achieve prosperous results. She lost her home through hate. She attracted the person she most hated. How she attracted alcoholics. How she attracted burns on her hand. How negative use of the Law of Attraction destroyed a marriage, generated heart trouble and produced two hated bosses. How he attracted ill health, then death. How to attract happy results. How she attracted wealth after having experienced poverty. How she attracted a happy marriage. How he attracted happiness, prosperity and contentment after having attracted tragedy. How a job, home, furniture, boat, sports car, and freedom from indebtedness came to him. How you can use the Law of Attraction and prosper.

What the Promised Land means to you. The success power of preparation. How preparing, then waiting, worked for the author. The first step in Joshua's success plan: Arise, do something. Jehovah's success commands to the Hebrews. How he paid off a huge indebtedness and began to make $200,000 a year. How a woman in Australia prospered herself and others. Why you must arise and do something.

The second step in Joshua's success plan: Use your "no" and "yes" mind powers. How a businessman overcame strong barriers and entered his Promised Land. The "no" power saved him from bankruptcy. He attracted a millionaire investor through the "yes" power. The third step in Joshua's success plan: Perform inner and outer cleansing. The fourth step in Joshua's success plan: Dissolve barriers with victorious words and divine promises. How he warded off financial ruin, and regained his health and financial success. The fifth step in Joshua's success plan: Give thanks. A special thanksgiving prosperity formula. The prospering power of a "faith offering." The prospering power of a "thank offering." How her home life, marriage, and career were vastly improved. The basic secret for getting into your Promised Land. Their immediate rewards in the Promised Land.

How to meet an "impossible" situation successfully. How this method overcame obstacles for the author. How they used their "no" power and persisted into success. How an alcoholic made a comeback. How a serviceman turned his assignment into a good one. What they did in the face of danger. Their strange plan for victory. How he changed jobs and tripled his salary. How a business executive prospered her company. How she lost weight. How he got a better job. The all-conquering power of words. How to prosper through the atomic power of your words. How they obtained bountiful results. How her words helped a relative at a distance. How prosperity statements spoken in a loud voice manifested a much-needed job. She heard the walls of Jericho fall down. How to take a curse off your problems. How to remove a curse from your life. How to remove a curse from the lives of others. How to remove a curse others may have placed upon your life. You can remove a curse with a blessing. How she turned a disappointment into a blessing. How he removed a curse and prospered. Prosperity and fame in the end.

The basic law of prosperity. What to do when things get tight. How she went from a "frightfully tight" to a bountiful Christmas season. He

prospered, guided, and healed them. How to avoid the high price of no results. How to have time for everything. How to avoid hurry and prosper. The benefits of psychological warfare.

Joshua on the success power of change. How change is a success power. Hold fast and fail, let go and succeed. How to recognize change at work. He was forced into a change that brought success. Things that drop away from you are a part of your success. How to meet change nonresistantly and prosper. How the author's life improved through change. How they prospered in the Promised Land. How you can prosper through change.

Introduction....

FROM LIMITATION TO ABUNDANCE
THE AUTHOR'S INVITATION TO YOU!

From limitation to abundance: Others have traveled this path and so can you! The results that have been obtained by those who have used the prosperity methods described in this book are almost too numerous to recite, but here are a few:

After having experienced much personal tragedy, an Ohio businessman attracted new happiness, prosperity and contentment. After having despaired of ever marrying again, a widow entered into a successful new marriage. After a long period of financial limitation, a businessman gained freedom from indebtedness. He soon had his heart's desires: A new job, home, furnishings, a boat and sports car. In Australia, a woman was able to remodel her home and to buy a beach house. Her sister used the same prosperity methods and soon went on a trip around the world!

1

She then shared her prosperity secrets with a friend, who used them and got a much larger income. She also witnessed the happy engagement of her shy daughter to one of the town's most prominent citizens. A businessman went from the brink of bankruptcy to total affluence. A California businessman, who had gone broke in one business, met a millionaire who helped him go on to a grand success in another business. Still another West Coast businessman warded off financial ruin and gained satisfying new success. He also regained his health.

A new job, home and boy friend all came to a young Louisiana woman. The relief from previous strain over her daughter's affairs caused this girl's mother to experience a physical healing. She then celebrated by taking a trip abroad. A college girl stopped seeing a much older divorced father, and happily finished college—to the vast relief of her family. The way opened for a poor boy to get an education and prosper.

A penniless, divorced mother was suffering from job insecurity, painful health problems, and a house full of "problem children." First, she went on to a secure job. Next, one of the older children enlisted in the Armed Forces, while another obtained part-time work. All of them settled down emotionally. As this mother persisted in using the prosperity methods found in this book, she was surprised to inherit an *entire* estate from a distant relative. It consisted of a house, car, furniture, jewelry, stocks, and a mink coat. As the financial strain disappeared, so did her health problems. Her life literally went from the ridiculous to the sublime.

From limitation to abundance. Yes, it is still possible— even in these times. It has happened to others, and it can happen to you. So read on. . . .

HOW THE MILLIONAIRES OF THE BIBLE
CAN HELP YOU

As though it were an incredible idea, a Texas oilman recently exclaimed, "You mean there are *millionaires* in the Bible? Wow!" He then rushed out to buy my first two books on the subject, *The Millionaires of Genesis*[1] and *The Millionaire Moses*.[2]

Yes, the Bible is the finest prosperity textbook that has ever been written! The great people of the Bible had no psychological hang-ups on the subject of prosperity or success being a part of their spiritual heritage. They intuitively knew that true prosperity has a spiritual basis: That success that is achieved through spiritual methods leads to an enduring success. The word "gold" appears at least four hundred times in the Bible, and you will find more than four thousand promises of the blessings that can be yours in its pages.

Indeed, the Bible is "loaded" with millionaires! You have probably regarded Abraham, Isaac, Jacob, Joseph and Moses as great spiritual leaders of their time — which they were. But they also became millionaires, both literally and figuratively.

In fact, many of our present-day millionaires could hardly conceive the affluent life style of the millionaires of the Bible — with their vast flocks, huge land holdings, large

---

1. Catherine Ponder, (Marina del Rey, Calif.: DeVorss & Co., 1976).
2. Catherine Ponder, (Marina del Rey, Calif.: DeVorss & Co., 1977).

families, and unlimited staff of servants. It was a gracious, leisurely way of life that might be difficult even for a person of wealth to maintain at today's prices. The frantic, hard-work, competitive consciousness of modern man can hardly imagine it. Yet the abundant prosperity consciousness — which the millionaires of the Bible symbolize — is still available to us today.

A millionaire is generally regarded as one who has a million dollars or more. In its root the word "millionaire" also means "abundance and happiness." That suggests that you, too, can experience greater abundance and happiness, even to the point of unlimited wealth, as you discover and use "the dynamic laws of prosperity" that were used by the ancient millionaires.

The word "wealth" means "to fare well." Your wealth encompasses your well-being on all levels of life. Your health, prosperity, happiness, peace of mind, spiritual awareness, and growth into expanded good are all your wealth. Indeed, your potential wealth includes all the good your soul desires. As you open your mind to claim this abundance, your life takes on more and more of the blessings you desire, so that you "fare well" or become wealthy.

And such an expanded prosperity consciousness is a necessity in this age of increasing economic demands. Rising prices, "inflationary recessions" and uncertain political and economic world conditions are an indication that you must raise and expand your consciousness to a new level of universal supply. In this book, the colorful Joshua shows you how.

HOW THE MILLIONAIRES OF THE BIBLE
HAVE PROSPERED THE AUTHOR

I am writing about the millionaire, Joshua, from the study of my Palm Springs, California home. Through the window I can view the rich tropical beauty of blooming bougainvillea, oleanders, roses and petunias surrounded by citrus and palm trees in a setting of bright sunshine. Towering over all this beauty is the majestic San Jacinto Mountain that changes in color throughout the day, beginning with pale pink at dawn and progressing through many shades to deep purple at dusk.

As I daily view the beauty to be found in this world-famous oasis of wealth, glamor and gaiety known as Palm Springs, it is hard to believe that only a few years ago I was still living in a furnished apartment in Texas; that somewhat earlier I had resided in only one room in Alabama; and that my childhood had been spent in a humble rented house in a poverty-stricken area of the Deep South.

Yes, it has been quite a journey from that deprived childhood to the colorful *Social Register* life style I now experience in America's foremost desert resort. These blessings are blended with a busy life of writing, lecturing and serving mankind as a nondenominational minister.

It is gratifying to finally be working for the joy of it — not only to make a living, but also to make a life — and to share generously with people everywhere all that life has taught me.

How did such a drastic improvement in my life style come about? And what can it mean to you?

There has been no flash flood of supply. Instead, I attribute my expanded good to a gradual acquaintance with the millionaires of the Bible, and the prosperity secrets I have learned from them. I first launched forth on this fascinating study more than twenty years ago while living in one room in Alabama. During the severe recession of 1958, I taught to a group of business people a prosperity class which was so successful that it led to the writing of my first book, *The Dynamic Laws of Prosperity.*[3] Soon afterwards, I began researching the material for *The Millionaires of Genesis*[4] — my first book in "The Millionaires of the Bible" series.

It was startling to me then, as it is to many people now, to realize that there were so many millionaires in the Bible. It was even more surprising to discover that no theologian, minister or inspirational writer had *ever* researched the prosperity secrets of the Bible's millionaires, and then dared to write about them so that all mankind could prosper from their ancient wisdom. This one discovery opened up an exciting new field of research and writing to me. Of course, my research also expanded my own thinking which, in turn, gradually enriched my life in countless ways.

WHAT JOSHUA'S SUCCESS CAN MEAN TO YOU

I can certainly identify with Joshua, who went from slave to millionaire, and you probably can, too. He was born into Egyptian bondage where he experienced limitation of every kind. While still a slave in Egypt, Joshua learned about the power of thought. This gave him hope for a better way of

3. Catherine Ponder, (Marina del Rey, CA: DeVorss & Co., rev. ed. 1985).
4. Ponder (Marina del Rey, CA: DeVorss & Co., 1976).

life. Later, while in the wilderness, he learned and absorbed much from the masterful Moses, one of the Bible's earlier millionaires.

After being freed from Egyptian bondage and escaping to the wilderness, Joshua acted as a spy in the Promised Land. There he surveyed its vast wealth and unlimited potential. Yet he had to wait another forty years in the wilderness of Paran before being allowed to permanently enter the Promised Land.

Joshua made this frustrating period of waiting a time of learning, planning and preparing. Then when the opportunity came, he was ready to go in, claim the Promised Land for his followers, and settle there.

It is an exciting story, and one that is symbolic of the vast good that can await you in your own life, as you follow through on Joshua's success secrets that are explained in this book.

WHAT JOSHUA'S SUCCESS HAS MEANT
TO THE AUTHOR

I can pinpoint in my own life the three phases that Joshua went through in claiming his good:

After being freed from the limitations of my early life spent in a poverty-stricken area of the South (I think of that as my Egyptian bondage period), I, too, went through a long period of learning, planning, preparing, then waiting, first in Alabama and later in Texas (my wilderness period), before I was finally able to enter my long desired Promised Land here in Southern California.[5]

5. I do not mean to imply that Alabama or Texas are wilderness areas. They are both beautiful states. However, I experienced an inner

I first visited the Palm Springs area—which has a terrain similar to that of the Promised Land—a decade before I was able to settle in the vicinity. Yet like Joshua, the area haunted me during that ten year period and I was unable to forget it. So I, too, learned, planned, prepared and waited in my own wilderness of Paran. The word "Paran" appropriately symbolizes a place of much earnest searching after Truth. This searching occurs when one becomes sufficiently convinced that abundant good is his heritage, and then grows into the conscious understanding and dominion that are necessary in order to go in and claim his Promised Land.

Now as I happily take walks in the old movie-colony neighborhood of Palm Springs where I live, I like to reflect upon how it is presently possible for me to reside in an area that is permeated by vast wealth and lavish tropical beauty. To be able to live in this environment did not come to me as a result of inherited wealth, from the receipt of some financial windfall, through knowing "the right people," by "playing politics," or because of supposed family prestige or connections. Mine had none.

No! My life amid the millionaire consciousness that permeates this desert environment is the result of the prosperity secrets I have learned—and am still learning—from the millionaires of the Bible. Over and over they used "the dynamic laws of prosperity" to benefit themselves and their followers, and you and I can, too!

---

wilderness period in my growth during the phases of my life spent in those areas.

A PROSPERITY INVITATION TO YOU

The reason I relate my own experiences is because I am convinced that if I can use the prosperity secrets found in this book to succeed, *anyone can!* Even if you, too, had humble beginnings, then encountered a long climb to survive financially, emotionally and career-wise; even if you, too, had some heartbreaking setbacks along the way, there is still hope. *To use invisible ideas to produce visible results—from the inside out—is the only way to permanently prosper and succeed in life.* Joshua proved it and so can you.

As you study Joshua's success secrets and apply them to your own life, I invite you to join me in traveling the path from limitation to abundance. It is a path that began for Joshua as a slave in Egypt and victoriously ended for him as Premier of the Promised Land! For me it is proving to be a fascinating lifetime journey.

I also invite you to write me about your experiences as increased good comes your way. This book begins where *The Millionaire Moses* book concluded: with the Hebrews in view of their long-awaited Promised Land. Moses' charge to Joshua and the Israelites had been: "Behold, I have set the land before you; go in and possess the land which Jehovah sware unto your fathers, to Abraham, to Isaac, and to Jacob, to give unto them and to their seed after them." (Deuteronomy 1:8) This present book, along with others in this continuing series on "The Millionaires of the Bible," provides you with an entire success course—one that is filled with ancient success secrets from the past, the kind not always found in our modern success courses.

And now turn quickly to the pages of this book and learn how Joshua went from slave to millionaire. *His progress is symbolic of all the rich blessings that await you as you also open your mind to prosperity, and deliberately travel the path from limitation to abundance!*

                                                    Catherine Ponder
P.O. Drawer 1278
Palm Desert, California, 92261
U.S.A.

FROM SLAVE TO MILLIONAIRE

— Chapter 1 —

One of the most exciting stories of all times is the story of Joshua, who went from slave to millionaire. What is even more exciting is that you, too, can go from "slave to millionaire" as you use Joshua's prosperity methods to rise out of limitation into abundance! Before considering the specific prosperity laws he used, which are described beginning with Chapter 2, let us first view the over-all success secrets we can learn from his long, eventful life:

The multitalented Joshua has been described by historians as a servant to Moses, spy, soldier, saviour of the Hebrews, a statesman, and saint. He became Israel's premier, a mature warrior, and a perfect knight. He has been described as an elusive figure early in his life, as a successful initiate, a man of honor, a student of the great Moses, a learned man, a strict leader, an outstanding general, and a

highly-evolved soul who fulfilled a divine mission of millionaire proportions! Here is how it all began:

JOSHUA'S LIFE—PART I—AS A SLAVE IN EGYPT

Joshua's Prosperous Background

Joshua had a prosperous background. He was born in
Egypt in the 13th Century B.C. There, during the first forty-
five years of his life, he was exposed to the vast wealth of the
richest country of the ancient world.

Joshua was surrounded by an aura of prosperity even at
birth. The name "Joshua" not only means "Jehovah's help,
salvation, triumph, victory and deliverance," it also means
"Jehovah makes rich." For Joshua this was prophetic because the events of his life show that with Jehovah's help,
Joshua became a millionaire and his descendants became
rich beyond compare.

That Joshua radiated an aura of prosperity, even at birth,
is also shown in the fact that he was the son of Nun, a name
which means "durable prosperity" or "eternal increase."
Joshua was born of the tribe of Ephraim which means "very
productive" or "doubly fruitful." With such a prosperous
background, it is not surprising that Joshua was destined to
become a millionaire as well as to bring "eternal increase"
to his followers in both inner and outer ways.

Even as a slave in Egypt, Joshua had enjoyed the promi-
nence of being a descendant of the great national hero,
Joseph. The memory of the billionaire Joseph was still revered by the Egyptians because, as their illustrious prime

minister, Joseph had saved them from starvation in an earlier era. He had brought vast riches and honor to their country, and his legend lived on four hundred years later. Thus, Joshua's prestige was enhanced, while humbly serving the Egyptians, by the overwhelming success and popularity of his famous ancestor.

Joshua's Prosperity Was Linked to That of Jesus

The prosperous significance of the name Joshua is further shown in the fact that "Joshua" in Hebrew is identical with the name "Jesus" in Greek. The humble carpenter from Nazareth later became Lord of Plenty as He multiplied the loaves and fishes, turned ordinary water into priceless wine, and manifested tax money from the fish's mouth.

That Joshua developed a prosperity consciousness similar to that of the powerful Jesus became more and more evident as the events of Joshua's life unfolded. Both Joshua and Jesus symbolize the divinity within man that is never poor. Whereas Joshua set out to conquer the Promised Land, centuries later Jesus set out to conquer the world and free it of limitation.

The Egyptians' Secret Name for Success Was Passed on to the Hebrews

It is interesting that both names, Joshua and Jesus were derived from the word "Jehovah" which means *"I AM THAT I AM."* This mystical phrase, which is filled with success power, was not a new one to Joshua. The Egyptians felt there was such great power in the name *"I AM"* (which means God *within*) that this phrase appeared upon the walls of every Egyptian temple. Both Moses and Joshua became familiar with that sacred name during their years in Egypt. Later the term *"I AM"* was called "the song of Moses" because it was considered his secret text for success.

The Hebrews used the term *"I AM"* so much that they became known as "the people of the *I AM*." They considered the term *"I AM"* the lost word of power which, when released in meditation and through spoken decrees, could perform miracles in an instant. That they stirred up the God-power within them through dwelling upon the words *"I AM"* is indicated in the vast wealth and great power that came to them, after their arrival in the Promised Land. This was quite a contrast to their earlier history as runaway slaves.

Joshua's Song of Success

Whereas the phrase *"I AM,"* meaning the God-power *within*, had been "the song of Moses" and his secret text for success, it was the expanded phrase *"I AM THAT I AM,'* meaning the *universal* God-power, that had been "the song of Joshua" and his secret text for success.

That Joshua's name meant *"I AM THAT I AM"* was prophetic of the widespread influence he was to have upon the Hebrews for generations to come. It became Joshua's mission to call often upon that universal God-power, *"I AM THAT I AM,"* to help unify the Hebrews so that they could enter their Promised Land and enjoy its vast benefits.

Whereas, Moses helped teach the Hebrews that they had a power *within* them that would deliver them from their bondage and wilderness experiences, it was Joshua who helped them externalize that inner power and use it in a *universal* way to go forth and claim their Promised Land, settle there permanently, and pass on the vast wealth they generated within and without to future generations.

How You Can Use This "Song of Success"

What is the practical meaning of those terms *"I AM"* and *"I AM THAT I AM?"* How can you use them to solve problems and to prosper?

For Yourself: Go alone, close your eyes, and speak over and over the phrase, *"I AM,"* which means God *within.* Soon you will feel your whole being filled with a sense of power you had not previously known.

Then dwell on such phrases as *"I am love," "I am health," "I am prosperous," "I am peace."* Try for just one week always using the words *"I AM"* positively toward the good you wish to experience. The results can amaze you. Say to your problems: *"I AM hath sent me."* This opens the way to surmount all difficulties.

The story is told of how the young George Washington used his *"I AM"* power to succeed. As early as the age of 12 he insisted, "I am going to marry a beautiful woman. I am going to be one of the wealthiest men in the land. I am going to lead the army of my colony. I am going to rule the nation which I help to create."

For Others: For the problems of other people declare: *"I AM THAT I AM is mightily at work for you now."* Through use of those words (meaning *universal* God power), you grip a handle of power that will produce outer results.

Also if you have felt the stirring of *inner* power by meditating upon *"I AM,"* but have not obtained the *outer* results desired, begin to affirm *"I AM THAT I AM"* in your meditations. This opens the way for visible results.

A businesswoman learned about the *"I AM"* power for success at a time when she was in very bad health. In spite of fine medical treatment, there seemed little hope for her to get well. It was in desperation that she began to meditate and affirm daily: *"I AM THAT I AM is healing me now."* When people asked, "How are you feeling?" she replied, "I am feeling fine." As she said it over and over she began to feel better. Her health is now perfect.

These mystical phrases can become your song of success, too!

Joshua's Awareness of the Prosperity Laws

We see "the dynamic laws of prosperity" being used over and over in the Bible. While still a slave in Egypt, and later, upon entering the wilderness, Joshua became aware of some of those universal prosperity principles.

Like his prominent ancestors, Joshua was also destined to use the prosperity law of release, and leave the material wealth of Egypt behind. Along with thousands of his kinsmen, Joshua made a dramatic departure out of Egypt under the able leadership of the magnificient Moses.

Like Abraham in Babylon, and like Moses in Egypt, Joshua was destined to leave the outer material wealth of Egypt in order to develop an inner, metaphysical consciousness of prosperity—which would prosper him far more lavishly on a permanent basis than material wealth alone ever could have done.

An inner consciousness of wealth includes all of the vast benefits of material wealth, but much more: peace, health and plenty always accompany an inner consciousness of supply. There is no fear of loss or sense of burden because one looks to God for guidance and supply, rather than looking to people or conditions.

The prosperity consciousness that Joshua began developing in a barren wilderness was to lavishly enrich his kinsmen for many generations to come. That same lavish prosperity consciousness—one that is not controlled by inflation, recession or economic fluctuations on the world scene—is still available to you today as you become aware of it and make the inner effort to develop it!

This prosperity meditation has helped many people to do so:

"I do not depend upon persons or conditions for my prosperity. God is the source of my supply, and God provides his own amazing channels of supply to me now.

"My prosperity now comes to me from expected channels in expected ways. My prosperity also comes to me from unexpected channels in unexpected ways. From all points of the universe, rich supply comes to me now."

While still serving as a slave in Egypt, Joshua had observed Moses' use of the prosperity law of persistence when

Moses dealt with the powerful King Pharaoh. Moses had insisted over and over "Let my people go" until it had finally happened. (Exodus 5:1; 7:16; 8:1, 20; 9:1, 13; 10:3)

Joshua had learned *the prospering power of looking to God for guidance, protection and supply.* He had been in that great throng of perhaps two million who left Egypt by night and witnessed Jehovah's incredible protection and deliverance when the pursuing Egyptians drowned in the sea while trying to recapture the Hebrews.

Joshua had been on hand when the hungry, thirsty Hebrews reached the barren wilderness. He observed the prosperity laws used by Moses to miraculously provide water from the rock and manna from heaven. He observed the unusual way the Hebrews were clothed in that desolate place. He was among those whom Moses later reminded:

"Thy raiment waxed not old upon thee, neither did thy foot swell these forty years."[1]
                                    (Deuteronomy 8:4)

Joshua was among those who began putting into practice prosperity's Ten Commandments, as given by Jehovah to Moses, soon after arriving in the wilderness.

Joshua observed Moses' belief that opulence was their heritage, even in that barren wilderness. This became apparent when Moses followed Jehovah's instructions and ordered the construction of a portable sanctuary worth more than $400,000 and filled it with priceless gold, silver and brass.

Joshua observed the bejeweled clothes designed for the high priest of Israel, described as "garments for glory and

---

1. Bible passages quoted herein are from the American Standard Version of the Holy Bible unless otherwise indicated.

for beauty." (Exodus 28:2) "Skillfull workmen" equivalent
to our modern designers and tailors, had designed those
elegant garments of fine linen in brilliant colors set in gold,
worn with emeralds, diamonds and other precious stones.
(Exodus 28:6) Such an incredible display of lavish beauty
and wealth in one's surroundings in a desert place doubtless left its mark on Joshua's expanding awareness of Universal Abundance and his access to it.

JOSHUA'S LIFE—PART II—IN THE WILDERNESS

Moses Was Joshua's Prosperity Teacher

The events of Joshua's life indicate that he became a
highly developed man and a successful initiate. How did
this happen?

In the wilderness, Joshua was privileged to study with one
of the greatest prosperity teachers of all times—Moses!
Joshua shared the confidence of Moses as he worked side by
side with him.

Legend states that Moses established a mystery school in
the wilderness where he gave a few chosen initiates certain
oral teachings, which were never written, but were passed
on from one generation to the next by word of mouth.
These instructions were in the form of philosophical keys
based upon metaphysical interpretation, some of which are
still known and taught today.

The first five books of the Bible, attributed to Moses'
authorship, contain these fascinating metaphysical keys for
prosperous living. They are found there in both literal
and allegorical form. The most obvious prosperity principles taught during that era are found in this book, in the

companion book, *The Millionaire Moses*,[2] and in other books in this continuing "Millionaires of the Bible" series.

Where did Moses learn the mystical keys to success which he passed on to Joshua? As an Egyptian prince, Moses had been instructed in all of the secrets of the Egyptian priesthood, which included instructions in metaphysics. The word "Moses" in an esoteric Egyptian sense meant "one who had been admitted to the mystery schools of wisdom." Legend states that when Moses set up the twelve tribes of Israel in the wilderness, he established his secret school of wisdom in their midst called "the tabernacle mysteries."

In any event, while still a prince of Egypt, Moses had received instructions in the secret teaching that "substance" is the key to all wealth. His knowledge of the prospering power of substance had been powerful enough to help Moses free the Hebrews from the feared, materialistic Pharaoh.

Joshua had been among those Hebrews whom Moses had taught how to dwell upon "substance" as the basis of their supply, so that they were able to survive the barren wilderness for forty years, and travel to the edge of their Promised Land.

Joshua learned well from his prosperity teacher, Moses, the secret that substance was the source of all wealth. This is shown in the daring way he led the Hebrews into the Land of Canaan, when he became their leader.

**Why the Promised Land of Canaan
Symbolized Unlimited Wealth**

No wonder the Hebrews were so interested in getting into their Promised Land of Canaan!

2. Ponder, (Marina del Rey, Calif.: DeVorss & Co., 1977).

First, Jehovah had made Abraham, the father of the Hebrews, a millionaire promise:

> "I will give unto thee, and to thy seed after thee, the land of thy sojournings, *all* the land of Canaan, for an everlasting possession."
>
> (Genesis 17:8)

Second, the word "Canaan" metaphysically means "realm of substance." The Hebrews were trying to gain an understanding of substance as the key to all wealth and how to manifest that wealth as visible results.

It was Joshua's destiny to lead the Hebrews into their Promised Land of Canaan—"realm of substance"—because he symbolizes the executive power of the mind that goes in and gets things done. The later events of his life indicate that he did this.

That substance is the key to all wealth is a secret prosperity teaching that has been known since ancient times. *Those who have grasped its meaning have enjoyed its prospering power over and over.*

At first it may have seemed a strange idea to the Hebrews that substance was the basis of all wealth. That they learned well this age-old secret is evidenced by the fact that in the Land of Canaan, they enjoyed unparalleled wealth for many centuries. During that era they also developed a group prosperity consciousness so strong that it has endured among their descendants even to this day!

As you gain an inner hold on substance as the key to all wealth, you, too, can move forward into the Land of Canaan—that "realm of substance" that is your rich Promised Land of unlimited supply.

How a Housewife Prospered Herself and Others

The better you understand the nature of substance out of which comes all wealth, the better you will be able to bring forth whatever you desire, and the better every phase of your life will be!

The word "substance" means "that which stands under" all visible forms of life. It has been described as "the body of God" out of which all things are formed through the action of the mind. It begins to manifest as visible results for you when you recognize it and call upon it for help.

A housewife from Texas wrote:

"I have been using this statement for myself and for others: *'Divine Substance is the one and only reality in my (your) life now, and Divine Substance is producing perfect results.'*

"The results for myself: My husband and I were able to take our first vacation trip abroad in three years. I received news that I would begin receiving a gift of $100 per month. My husband released an old dissatisfying job and went on to something better.

"The results for others: Two people obtained jobs. A businessman received an unexpected check for $1,200. Another promptly received a letter that had held up the probating of a will. An employee got two promotions within a week and a half. Two people won court cases, one for money, the other for land. A secretary received a $100 a month raise. A widow went from 200 down to 147 pounds. A parent was relieved of a heavy emotional burden. A businessman, hospitalized for a kidney operation, was told no operation was needed, and was released.

Another man had been hospitalized for a heart condition, but further tests revealed it had cleared up."

The Significance of Joshua Acting as Moses' Servant

Moses trained Joshua just as Jesus later trained the twelve disciples. Joshua's special function in the wilderness was to carry out the commands of his teacher, Moses. He did so with humility, unswerving loyalty and devotion. His success in doing so led to these further responsibilities:

When he was selected by Moses to rout the Amaleks (Exodus 17), Joshua defeated them in a brilliant victory in Sinai.[3] He was placed in charge of the tabernacle meetings and he was appointed a member of the tribal representatives sent in to survey Canaan. That Joshua had a prosperity consciousness is indicated in the report he gave on the Promised Land when he returned from spying there. His loyalty led to his eventual succession of Moses as the esteemed Premier of Israel.

That Joshua was so loyal to the commands of Moses has special significance for you and for me:

The possession of the Promised Land was conditioned upon complete obedience—to the laws of mind action. Moses symbolized *knowledge* of these laws—the inner laws of prosperity and success which function through the mind. Whereas, Joshua symbolizes *love* of these laws and their use.

Like Moses, you can claim freedom from a great deal of bondage in your life through gaining a knowledge of the inner laws of prosperity. That *knowledge* can lead you to the very edge of your Promised Land of unlimited supply.

---

3. See Ponder, *The Millionaire Moses* (Marina del Rey, Calif.: DeVorss & Co., 1977) Chapter 5.

But it takes Joshua's *love* of the laws of prosperity, and a fearless use of them day in and day out, to free you completely from your wilderness periods, and to carry you forward into the land of abundance.

Perhaps you've heard this old joke: "What is the quickest way to get to Carnegie Hall?" asked a visitor on the streets of New York.

"Practice, practice, practice," came a musician's reply.

There is a mystic saying, "There must be an *inworking* before there can be an *outworking.*" Yes, there must be an "inworking" of the laws of prosperity in your thoughts, feelings and understanding before there can be an "outworking" of prosperous results in your life. The "inworking" takes patient persistence, the kind Joshua exhibited in the wilderness as he faithfully carried out Moses' commands. But the lasting benefits enjoyed by him, and by his followers for many generations afterwards, made the process a worthwhile one for them, and an inspiration to all who study their success methods.

How Joshua's Love of the Law Helped the Author

When I recently looked at some notes of research I had done on Joshua ten years ago while still living in Texas, I realized that that period was certainly an appropriate one for me to be ferreting out his success secrets.

Like the Children of Israel, I was in the midst of my own wilderness period. Even though I had written the best selling book, *The Dynamic Laws of Prosperity,*[4] and had been prospered by its philosophy to a degree, I was still working

---

4. Ponder (Marina del Rey, CA: DeVorss & Co., 1962).

hard to develop a new ministry from "financial scratch," and to prosper personally. During this period I was also trying to emotionally survive the sudden death of my late husband, and there were other tests. My Promised Land seemed far, far away.

It did not help to ask, "Where is my good?" or "Why don't 'the dynamic laws of prosperity' work for me more?"

I discovered that it was only when I decided that I loved the laws of prosperity so much that I would continue to use them anyway, that they began to "work" for me personally in greater degrees, just as they were working for thousands of my readers. That became the turning point to far better results for me than at any previous period.

Knowledge of the laws of mind action (Moses) gives you confidence and power. It urges you to go forward. But that is not enough. Love of the laws of mind action (Joshua) helps you to proceed. *Although Joshua spent forty-five years in the negative conditions of Egyptian slavery, and another forty years in the wilderness, he never let those experiences affect him adversely. He was learning, growing, preparing, planning for better things all that time!*

Too many people who read self-help books stop with Moses — *knowledge* of the laws of mind action. Then they wonder why they do not get results from their study. It takes *love* of those laws — and persistent use of them — as reflected in the life of Joshua — to cross over into one's Promised Land.

A fan once wrote me, "I have read *all* of your books. Now what do I do?"

"Practice, dear. Practice."

I know from personal experience that to do so will bring satisfying results in "the fullness of time." It is an evolving process, as Joshua discovered.

JOSHUA'S LIFE—PART III—IN THE PROMISED LAND

Joshua as the Prosperous Saviour of the Hebrews

Joshua was 85 years of age when he assumed leadership of the Hebrews at Shittim in the land of Moab. This was the last place they encamped before passing over the Jordan to possess the land of Canaan. It had first been from the mountain of Moab that Jehovah had pointed out the Promised Land to Moses.

The word "Shittim" symbolizes resurrection into a new life. "Moab" symbolizes the possibilities of good in the external conditions of life. This is exactly what Joshua and his followers were ready for at this point: a new life and new good in the external conditions of their lives.

After forty-five years spent in Egyptian slavery, and another forty years with Moses in the wilderness, Joshua was "full of wisdom" (Deuteronomy 34:9) and well prepared for the divine commission that had been given him by Moses:

> "Be strong and of good courage, for you shall bring the Children of Israel into the land which I swore to give them; and I will be with you."
>
> (Deuteronomy 31:23)

Before his transition, Moses had bestowed a prosperity blessing upon these future millionaires. While looking out upon the Promised Land from Mount Nebo, Moses had described the lavish wealth that Joshua and his followers were to enjoy in Canaan:

"Bless Jehovah, his substance . . .
Blessed of Jehovah be his land . . .
For the precious things of heaven, for the dew . . .
And for the precious things of the earth and the fullness thereof . . .
For they shall suck the abundance of the seas . . .
And the hidden treasures of the sand.
And full with the blessing of Jehovah . . .
And in a land of grain and new wine . . .
Happy art thou, O Israel."

(Deuteronomy 33)

With Egypt and Mt. Sinai behind, the desert wilderness all around, and the Promised Land just ahead, Joshua was finally on his way. He entered the Promised Land in just three short days—after having waited forty years. What a story!

And what a saviour he was. His conquests and victories are symbolic of the conquests and victories that the laws of prosperity make possible to all who faithfully use them.

His success-charge had been:

"Only be strong and very courageous, to observe to do according to all the law, which Moses my servant commanded thee:

"Turn not from it to the right hand or to the left, that thou mayest have good success whithersoever thou goest.

"This book of the law shall not depart out of thy mouth, but thou shalt meditate thereon day and night,

that thou mayest observe to do according to all that is
written therein;

"For then thou shalt make thy way prosperous, and
then thou shalt have good success."

(Joshua 1:7, 8)

Joshua's Success As a Tribal Hero and Military Leader

Joshua's brillance as a soldier had first been witnessed at
Amalek, while he was still in the wilderness serving under
Moses' command. Now, as the newly appointed military
leader of Israel, he was on his own. Archaelogical evidence
indicates that it was during the 13th Century B.C. that
Joshua became a tribal hero and premier of all Israel.

The Book of Joshua is a story of war, a holy war. Historians feel that without its wars of conquest, Israel could not
have experienced its glorious destiny. Yet in all their achievements, the Hebrews realized that it was God who gave them
the victory. In their conquering hero, Joshua, they recognized something not of earth or time. They observed that he
lived in an awareness of God's presence as he often asked for
divine guidance. Joshua pointed out to them again and
again that loyalty to God alone would bring victory to
Israel. In his 110-year life span, Joshua spent only seven
years as a warrior in conquest of Canaan.

His actions as a soldier were those of directness, complete-
ness and speed. He knew that to make a start was half the
battle; that to win, you've got to be "goal-oriented." After a
start was made under Joshua's leadership, the campaign
proceeded rapidly. The invading Hebrews formed a single

army, the Promised Land was entered, Jericho was captured, and they entered the hill country. Next came the southern campaign, followed by one in the North. Then the task was completed. The entire land of Canaan had been conquered by Joshua's united army in the miraculously short span of seven years. "And the land had rest from war." (Joshua 11:23)

As a military leader, Joshua was a genius. He knew how to plan campaigns, discipline his forces, and use spies. He developed his own C.I.A. and F.B.I. He never stooped to pilfering or plunder. He was captain of the Lord's host, and has been described by one historian as "every inch a soldier and every inch a Christian." Many a general has closely studied Joshua's conquests of Canaan and tried to follow his strategy.

In spite of the fact that the Book of Joshua is a book of war, it is permeated by an intensely religious atmosphere. It reflects the sublime faith in Jehovah as the God of Israel, which Joshua instilled in his people. Joshua's divine mission, and the triumph of the mission, is related. Of course, Joshua's divine mission included the prosperity mission of leading the Hebrews out of a barren wilderness into their own Promised Land of abundance, and helping them to become established in it. During Joshua's era, the Hebrews appeared to be sustained by the unlimited power of heaven because in all their achievements they gave God the victory!

Joshua As a Business Executive and Statesman

Following the conquest of Canaan, the Promised Land was then divided among the twelve tribes of Joshua and

Eleazar, Israel's high priest. Here we see the unselfish, mag-
nanimous statesmanship of Joshua in action. Under his
leadership:

a) The division of the land was completed.

b) The appointment of the cities of refuge was accomplished.

c) The arrangement of the Levitical order and service
was provided.

During this period, Joshua was busy getting things into
"divine order" in the Promised Land. It was all done with
precision and thoroughness. He had a job to do and he did
it to the finish without shirking his duty.

After the seven years of conquest, reconstruction began.
An orderly division of the land took place, tribe by tribe,
during this postwar era. After having gained the rich Promised Land, Joshua generously gave it for an inheritance to
Israel. (Joshua 11:23) He then happily spent the last eighteen years of his life among the Israelites as their beloved
leader and a prosperous man. The word "millionaire"
means "abundance and happiness." This he had accomplished for himself and for his new nation. The word
"wealth" means "well-being." This they experienced.

The Closing Prosperity Secrets of Joshua

As shown throughout this chapter, Joshua displayed the
basic qualities needed to succeed in his multifaceted career
on his way from slave to millionaire. Yet his most important
success secret was one that modern man has often overlooked in a frantic race toward success.

In his farewell address, Joshua gave his final success secret, which was a re-emphasis of the success charge that had been given him years earlier (Joshua 1:7,8); that of uncompromising loyalty to Jehovah if the newly found nation was to permanently survive and prosper:

"Choose you this day whom ye will serve . . . but as for me and my house, we will serve the Lord (the Law)."

(Joshua 24:15)

His followers listened well to his final piece of advice. The new nation continued to look to God for guidance and supply all the days that the elders lived who had served with Joshua.

Some historians have gone so far as to describe Joshua as a "saint." Of one thing we can be sure. His spiritual impact was tremendous:

a) He had been filled with the Spirit of God (Deuteronomy 34:9)

b) He had enjoyed the Presence of God. (Joshua 1:5, 6:27)

c) He had been permeated by the Word of God. (Joshua 1:8)

d) He had been obedient to the Will of God. (Joshua 5:14; Numbers 32:12)

His death at 110 was deeply mourned and his eminence was universally acknowledged.

That Joshua had accomplished well his prosperity mission is indicated in the fact that at his death, Joshua was buried in Timnath-serah which was located in the hill country of Ephraim. The name "Timnath-serah" means "fruitful, productive, a multiplying portion." The word "Ephraim" means "doubly fruitful."

Through his courage and daring, Joshua had made it possible for the Hebrews to settle down to fruitful, productive lives as a unified nation in their long-awaited Promised Land. Although the conquest was by no means complete, they were no longer despised, mistreated slaves in a foreign land, or insecure wanderers braving the challenges of a barren wilderness. In succeeding years, as they gained an ever-increasing understanding and control of the Land of Canaan—that rich "realm of substance" in which they had settled—they were destined to enjoy a "multiplying portion" of success. They were to become "doubly fruitful" to the point of unlimited wealth.

And this was as it should be. The blessings of health and prosperity, as a reward to the faithful, was a belief common to the Old Testament. Moses had repeatedly pointed this out to Joshua and the Hebrews in the Book of Deuteronomy. *If Israel were faithful, there would be no poor. Loyalty to Jehovah would bring inevitable prosperity.*

This was Joshua's final prosperity message and his greatest success secret. It is a message that still carries unlimited impact for prosperity and success to you and to me as we heed it today.

And now go quickly to Chapter 2 and begin discovering the *specific* success methods that Joshua employed for all that he accomplished step by step. Those same simple techniques are available to you, too. As you get busy using them, you can also go from "slave to millionaire" as you rise out of limitation into a far greater abundance than you have ever known before!

SUMMARY

1. In the process of his growth from slave to millionaire, Joshua has been described as a servant to Moses, spy, soldier, a mature warrior, a successful initiate, a man of honor, a learned man, a strict leader, an outstanding general, saviour of the Hebrews, the first premier of Israel, and a highly evolved soul who fulfilled a divine mission of millionaire proportions.

2. The multitalented Joshua had a prosperous background. He was born in Egypt, where for the first forty-five years of his life, he was exposed to its vast wealth. Joshua radiated an aura of prosperity even at birth. He was the son of Nun, a name which means "durable prosperity" or "eternal increase." He was born of the tribe of Ephraim which means "very productive" or "doubly fruitful."

3. The name "Joshua" means "Jehovah makes rich." This was prophetic since Joshua was destined to become a millionaire as well as to bring "eternal increase" to his followers in both inner and outer ways. They became rich beyond compare.

4. The name "Joshua" in Hebrew is identical with the name "Jesus" in Greek. Joshua and Jesus both symbolize the divinity within man that is never poor.

5. While still a slave in Egypt, and later upon entering the wilderness, Joshua became aware of universal prosperity principles, and began to use them. He observed the prosperity laws Moses used to miraculously provide water from the rock and manna from heaven for the Hebrews in the barren wilderness.

6. In the wilderness, Joshua studied with Moses, one of the greatest prosperity teachers of all times. Joshua was among those whom Moses taught to dwell upon "substance" as the foundation of all wealth.

7. The word "Canaan" metaphysically means "realm of substance." It was Joshua's destiny to get the Hebrews into their Promised Land of Canaan or to help them understand the "realm of substance' and how to claim it.

8. Moses symbolizes *knowledge* of the laws of mind action, the inner laws of success which function through the mind. Joshua symbolizes *love* of these laws and their use. The possession of the Promised Land was conditioned upon complete obedience to these laws. Joshua's function in the wilderness was to carry out the commands of his teacher, Moses. He did so with humility and loyalty, and this prepared him for possessing the Promised Land later—through complete obedience to the laws of mind action.

9. Joshua was 85 years of age when he assumed leadership of the Hebrews at Shittim in the land of Moab. "Shittim" symbolizes resurrection into a new life. "Moab" symbolizes the possibilities of good in the eternal conditions of life. Joshua and his followers were ready for a new life, and new good in the external conditions of their lives. Joshua had spent forty-five years in Egyptian slavery, and forty years with Moses in the wilderness.

10. After having waited forty years, Joshua entered the Promised Land in just three days. His conquests and victories in the Promised Land are symbolic of the conquests and victories that the inner laws of success make possible to all who faithfully use them.

11. In all their achievements, the Hebrews realized it was God who gave them the victory. Their theme had been: If Israel were faithful, there would be no poor. Loyalty to Jehovah would bring inevitable prosperity.

12. After having gained the rich Promised Land, Joshua generously gave it for an inheritance to Israel. After seven years of conquest, an orderly division of the land took place tribe by tribe. Joshua spent the last eighteen years of his life as their beloved leader and a very prosperous man. The word "millionaire" means "abundance and happiness." This he had accomplished for himself and his new nation.

THE PROSPERITY LAW OF
MENTAL ACCEPTANCE

— Chapter 2 —

Here is one of the most important success secrets there is
—one that can make you a millionaire both inwardly and
outwardly:

Psychologists say that you can have anything that you can
mentally accept, but that you must mentally accept it first.
If you cannot mentally accept it, you do not get your desired
good no matter what else you do!

*Upon learning the power of thought as a means of attain-
ing one's goals in life, people sometimes rush forth trying to
bring to pass that which they have not mentally accepted.
Even if they get what they want temporarily, they do not
keep it because they have not first developed a mental
acceptance of it.*

Perhaps this is why a gradual success is often more lasting. It leads to subconscious acceptance of that good degree

by degree. Over and over we learn from the millionaires of the Bible that *lasting success is a progressive process;* that it does not usually come in a flash flood of overnight wealth. After waiting forty years in the wilderness, Joshua entered the Promised Land in just three days. Then he had to claim that Promised Land degree by degree, step by step over a seven-year period.

WHY THE ABUNDANCE REPORT OF THE TWO PROSPEROUS-MINDED SPIES WAS REJECTED

Joshua gives you the formula for invoking the Prosperity Law of Mental Acceptance in the Book of Numbers, Chapters 13 and 14. The word "Numbers" means "in the wilderness," and it is during your wilderness periods that you will need most to use this same success law.

Soon after Joshua had been freed from Egyptian bondage, and early in his wilderness wanderings, he was one of the twelve spies commanded by Moses to slip into the Promised Land, investigate its conditions and bring back a report. One reason the spies were sent in was to help them mentally accept their long-awaited Promised Land by witnessing the great blessings that awaited them there.

The spies remained away so long — for forty days — that the Hebrews worried about their safety. When they finally returned, the spies gave conflicting reports. Joshua and Caleb were excited about what they found. Caleb enthusiastically said, "Let us go up at once and possess it, for we are well able to take it." (Numbers 13:30) The word "Caleb" means "bold and fearless." He described Canaan as a rich country and he even brought back proof of that abundance from the valley of Eshcol: figs, pomegranates, and a cluster of grapes so large that it had to be carried on a staff by two men! The word "Eshcol" symbolizes "great fruitfulness" or "abundant possibilities."

But, alas—Joshua and Caleb were the only prosperous thinkers in the group. Joshua was of the tribe of Ephraim which means "doubly fruitful." Caleb was of the tribe of Judah which symbolizes "increase and accumulation through praise."

The other ten spies gave a negative report: They claimed the land was filled with giants, walled cities and enemy forces, a place of famine and starvation.

The prosperous-minded Joshua tried to correct their false report:

"The land which we passed through . . . is an exceeding good land. If the Lord delight in us, then He will bring us into this land and give it to us; a land flowing with milk and honey."
(Numbers 14:7,8)

As for the hostile forces he said:

"Rebel not against Jehovah, neither fear ye the people of the land . . . Their defense is removed from over them. Jehovah is with us. Fear them not."
(Numbers 14:9)

But the people would not listen. Historians state that the Hebrews actually sat and wept all night over their plight— though their rich Promised Land was in plain view!

It is a pathetic example of people rejecting their good. With one bold stroke the Hebrews could have been in their long-dreamed-of Land of Abundance. Many of them actually wanted to return to the cursed limitations of Egyptian bondage, even though they could see their Promised Land awaiting them across the Jordan River.

Yet theirs was not such unusual behavior. Have you noticed that the moment a negative-minded person thinks he cannot get a thing, he seeks to knock it? There are times when man belittles the very blessings that he is reaching out for. He may even belittle the things he wants, ought to have, and could have. All because he has not yet got the nerve "to go up and possess it." In Chapters 3 and 4 of this book, Joshua will show us specifically how "to go up and possess it."

WHAT HAPPENS IF YOU DO NOT MENTALLY ACCEPT YOUR GOOD?

Psychologists say that when you think you have been rejected, you are in for a shock! *Your good never rejects you. Instead, you subconsciously reject it.*

Jehovah had assured the Hebrews repeatedly that He wanted them to have their Promised Land. He had used signs and wonders to get them out of the clutches of the powerful Pharaoh, and through the Red Sea. Not only had he kept them from starving, but He had even provided abundantly for them in the wilderness. Yet they still doubted. They would not accept their good.

When Jehovah realized that most of the Hebrews were not psychologically ready to go forward, He did what seemed a harsh thing. Yet it was only the working of impersonal law (Lord). Jehovah decreed that the ten negative-minded spies

would die on the spot, and that all of the griping Israelites who had wanted to go back to Egypt would die in the
wilderness. Those remaining would continue living in the
wilderness until the doubters had passed on. Then those
who could mentally accept the Promised Land would enter
it.

THE PROSPERITY LAW OF MENTAL ACCEPTANCE
WORKS THROUGH TWO STEPS

This is how the Prosperity Law of Mental Acceptance
works:

*Those who cannot mentally accept greater abundance
never experience it.* This explains why, after taking up the
study of prosperous thinking, some people get results while
others do not. Those who are successful in the use of the
Prosperity Law of Mental Acceptance are those who: (1)
dare to release the past, and (2) then mentally accept the
possibility of something better for themselves. Those who
hang on to the past and reject their longed-for good never
get it.

CAN YOU RELEASE LIMITATION?

Release of past limitation is often uncomfortable. Can
you do it? Are you so attached to old patterns of living that
you cannot get along without them? Are you emotionally
attached to a belief in lack and illness as a necessary part of
your life? Do you gain satisfaction from pitying yourself if
you have financial or health problems?

If you want to be healed, you must be willing to give up the sympathy and attention that come from being sick. In my book, *The Dynamic Laws of Healing,*[1] is the story of a woman who had been ill for some time. She asked for prayer help and began to experience a spiritual healing. This meant she could no longer claim the attention and sympathy that came to her when she was sick. When people began to say, "How well you look" it upset her. Finally she retorted, "I am not as well as you think!" And she went back to bed.

God can only do for you what He can do through your mental attitudes. Life demands much of the healthy person. Physicians know that much that passes for disease is man's attempt to escape life's responsibilities. The Master Physician-Psychologist, Jesus, sometimes inquired whether those seeking it wanted to be healed.

As a child I often accompanied my mother to visit a sick neighbor. She would be propped up in bed, surrounded by medicine bottles, in a dimly lit room. My mother spoke in low tones to this woman, who described her aches and pains in vivid details. A devoted husband hovered in the background and faithfully attended her.

After years of nursing his sick wife, this man suddenly passed away. His wife soon arose from her sick bed and went everywhere, visiting relatives and friends. She enjoyed the best health of her life and never had another sick day! When her devoted husband was no longer on hand to attend to her every whim, this woman apparently decided her illness wasn't worth it, so she quickly got well.

---

1. Ponder, (Marina del Rey, Calif.: DeVorss & Co., rev. ed. 1985).

HOW RELEASE OF A $5,000 LOSS BROUGHT $2,500
AND AN INHERITANCE

You must give up something to make way for the prosperity you want. It may be the release of something tangible such as worn-out possessions or worn-out relationships; or it may be the release of something intangible such as self-pity, bitterness, or the belief that you have had a hard time.

A professional man from Illinois bought $5,000 worth of stock in a company that went broke. Instead of immersing himself in self-pity and bitterness, this man released what had happened. He loosed it and let it go in his thoughts, words and actions. He refused to discuss it, and his daily meditation was: *"I fully and freely release. I loose and let go. I let go and grow. I let go and trust."*

This man soon received a gift of $2,500, and he was notified of a legacy that would more than compensate for his loss.

HOW RELEASE BROUGHT MUCH-NEEDED SECOND CAR
PLUS PEACE OF MIND AND FAMILY HAPPINESS

From Arizona a housewife wrote:

"For months I tried to demonstrate a new second car for our family. Our old one spent more time in the repair shop than on the street. I also felt it a good idea to sell part of a certain investment on which we could realize a profit and pay cash for the new car. My husband wouldn't hear of it.

"Well our old car kept going out. It seemed to want to get away from us as much as I wanted to get rid of it! After another large repair bill, it dawned on me that my husband was still emotionally attached to that old car. He had bought it in his home town, had driven it across country, and had enjoyed many adventures in it. I immediately spoke words of release and declared that the Divine Plan was manifesting for us and for that car.

"Within forty-eight hours my husband 'changed his mind.' We sold the investment at a profit, got an excellent trade-in for the old car, and purchased a new car that my husband can drive on his job as well as on camping trips. It will be a fine tax write-off so everyone is happy.

"I am continuing to speak words of release and I feel a vast inner freedom from old, unhappy memories. Practicing release is bringing peace and happiness into our lives. Regarding the tithe, I find the need to practice release there, too. It is not wise to keep God waiting for His tenth. He's one creditor we cannot afford to stall by stalling on our tithes. To do so 'stalls' our own good in so many ways. It is a joy to now be practicing release in so many fascinating ways."

HOW FORMING A VACUUM BROUGHT PETS, FURNISHINGS AND A NEW JOB

A young career woman wrote from Missouri:

"Since a vacuum is magnetic and attracts new good into one's life, I decided to practice release by forming a vacuum. I formed a vacuum and practiced release by giving away and selling possessions I no longer used. The results were amazing:

1. I created a vacuum to receive some goldfish I had long wanted. I found our old fishbowl, lovingly washed the years of dust from it, set in in the desired spot, and visualized beautiful fish swimming there. A friend traveled on a bus to bring me three goldfish the next week. Her explanation? Her brother was cleaning his aquarium, no longer needed those fish, and thought I might enjoy them. When my Mother heard of this, she made me a gift of two more fish—for company.

2. I created a vacuum because I desired a new chair for my bedroom. After releasing old possessions I no longer used, I visualized myself walking to that spot to sit in the chair, instead of having to sit on the bed. The new chair soon came in the form of a belated birthday gift from a friend.

3. In March I decided to create a vacuum by releasing my job for a week, because the dissatisfaction with it had become so acute. I arranged to take off the week, then remained at home practicing release of everything and everybody connected with that job. Each day I began to feel better, more hopeful and at peace. On the last day at home I felt in animated suspension. The tranquillity was delightful. After this, things changed within and without.

"The result was that I got a new and far better job in August, and life keeps improving. My apartment has been completely furnished easily. I have had one raise, and am about to receive a promotion. I am finally doing the things I have longed to do. Once I practiced letting go and letting God, my good rushed to me from every direction. I am just 21 years of age, and feel I have a great life before me—thanks to the miracle power of release."

HOW TO TAKE ONLY THE GOOD
FROM EACH EXPERIENCE AND LET THE REST GO

Your good has not rejected you but you may have rejected it by holding onto someone or some thing from the past. You hold on through resentment, hate, unforgiveness, criticism, emotional attachment. *That which you hold onto keeps you in your wilderness.* If you continue holding onto negative beliefs about your past and present, you will bog down in your wilderness experiences indefinitely. Your potential good will die.

On separate occasions, I talked with two divorced women. Both were leading confused, dissatisfying lives. They were in debt, overweight, and had job problems. One had a court case pending against her. In both instances, each of these women was confusing her life by retaining a compromising relationship with her former husband. One was still seeing two former husbands! They were foolishly proving that that which you hold onto keeps you in the wilderness.

Stop saying that you have had a hard time in life. Who hasn't—in one way or another? Stop talking about unhappy experiences. Cease trying to get sympathy. To continue doing so keeps you emotionally attached to hard experiences. As you continue to feed them emotionally, you keep them alive. There is no room in your thoughts and feelings for better experiences. Let go, release, loose, forgive, give up the past.

When you have reached the point where you take only the

good from each experience and let the rest go, your progress into a happy life will be swift and certain! Begin to mentally accept this by declaring: *"I take only the good from each experience. I let the rest go and my progress is swift, happy and certain."*

HOW RELEASE BROUGHT A BETTER JOB AND PAYMENT OF OLD DEBTS

A businessman from Michigan wrote:

"I decided to take only the good from an old experience and let the rest go by resigning from an unsatisfactory job. When I let go in this way, the doors of heaven opened to me. I have been prospered financially in both expected and unexpected ways. I have also been led to a far better job."

A widow, also from Michigan, wrote:

"I feel so much better since I have been practicing release of the past in connection with my husband's death, and the financial problems he left behind. This method has worked so well for me that all of the bills now have been paid off, except two or three small ones—thanks to the prospering power of release."

RELEASE BRINGS NEW JOB, HOME AND BOYFRIEND FOR THE DAUGHTER. IT BRINGS HEALING AND TRIP ABROAD FOR THE MOTHER

A mother from Louisiana wrote:

"Since that first desperate letter I wrote to you about the hostility that my only child expressed for me, I have practiced using prayers of release as you suggested. Here are the amazing results:

"She moved into her own beautiful little house which she is busy decorating. She has an excellent new job with her own private office. A new boyfriend has come into her life. As a result of the continued practice of release, a long-time infection of mine cleared up, and I took a trip abroad. I can hardly believe all the good that has come from the practice of release."

HOW RELEASE BRINGS FREEDOM FOR DAUGHTER FROM UNDERSIRABLE RELATIONSHIP

A mother from Ohio wrote:

"After twenty-two months, my daughter has stopped seeing a divorced man with two children. He was ill, unemployed and on welfare. You can imagine my concern since our daughter is a senior in college. In November you wrote me to release, let go and let God. I did and began to feel relaxed and at peace. On New Year's Eve they broke up. She is a completely different girl now: happy, cheerful, relaxed, making better grades and new friends her own age. Praise God for release."

HOW FORGIVENESS AND RELEASE BROUGHT HEALINGS AND MONEY

A housewife from Texas wrote:

"In our prayer group, we've had many healings, especially of cancer and heart conditions. These have resulted from our practice of prayers of forgiveness and release. We've had prosperity demonstrations in the form of winning of money, promotions, raises in pay, and the inheritance of money. These blessings came the same way — from the practice of forgiving and releasing everything and everybody that was no longer a part of the Divine Plan of our lives; of taking only the good from each experience, and letting the rest go. We never cease to be amazed at the miracles that result from doing this."

HOW TO START THINKING ABOUT YOUR LIFE THE WAY YOU WANT IT TO BE

The way to mentally accept your good is simply to change your point of view. Recognize that another set of circumstances is possible. Then dwell upon that possibility constantly. Declare often: *"I mentally accept the possibility of something better for myself. Vast improvement comes quickly in every phase of my life now. Every day in every way, things are getting better and better for me."*

Caleb recognized another set of circumstances as possible when he said:

"Let us go up at once and possess it, for we are well able to take it."

(Numbers 13:30)

Joshua recognized another set of circumstances as possible when he said to the complainers:

"The land which we passed through . . . is an exceeding good land . . . The Lord will bring us into this land and give it to us, a land flowing with milk and honey."

(Numbers 14:7,8)

Joshua did not claim he could take the Promised Land. He claimed God's help. It is significant that Moses had changed Joshua's name from "Hoshea" meaning "help" to "Joshua" meaning "God's help or salvation." (Numbers 13:8, 16; Deuteronomy 32:44) Joshua refused to be hypnotized by the walled cities and hostile forces. After releasing the past, he realized:

a) That other circumstances were possible.

b) He mentally pictured them.

c) He asked God's help in bringing them to pass.

In all these ways, he was invoking the Prosperity Law of Mental Acceptance.

HOW A POOR BOY GOT AN EDUCATION AND PROSPERED

There once was a young son of a farmer who had no training and little confidence in himself to succeed. His excuse was, "I never had a chance. Life has been hard on me. I am just a poor nobody."

Then he studied the power of thought and learned he was a spiritual being, who had been given dominion over a lavish universe, that he could claim his good through the action of the mind. This philosophy helped him to realize he was a "somebody" entitled to the opportunities, privileges and blessings of a good life.

He started claiming these blessings by saying, "Lord, I am ready." He decided that other sets of circumstances were possible. He asked God's help in claiming them. As he

did so, a wonderful thing happened: He was given a scholar-
ship to a leading university, where he became a student well
on the way to a prosperous new life. But it didn't happen as
long as he kept talking about what a hard life he had had.
*New and improved sets of circumstances are possible in
your life, too!* Decree they are possible, and ask God's help
by declaring often: *"Lord, I am ready."*

But be sure you mean it when you say, "I am ready."
Once the flow of good starts, you cannot stop it. You must
be willing to flow along with it. *You will receive at the level
of your acceptance, no more and no less.*

A minister wisely observed, "I have never seen a case of
unanswered prayer when the one asking was ready to receive
the answer."

HOW JOSHUA TURNED DELAY INTO A BLESSING

Although Joshua had personally witnessed the lavish
abundance of the Promised Land, he had to wait almost
forty years before going in to claim it. While he was waiting
for the complainers to die in the wilderness, Joshua might
have fretted incessantly. Instead he profited from the :xper-
ience because he used this period of delay as a time of
preparation and planning. He turned this delay into a
blessing.

Joshua was a master-planner. During those long years of
waiting in the wilderness, he worked out in detail how he
would take the Promised Land. He often went up on Mount
Nebo. From that high point, he quietly studied every detail
of the Land of Canaan. (See Chapter 3 in this book.)

The word "Nebo" means "height." It symbolizes the foresight that we must use in order to expand our world. You can go up on Mount Nebo by picturing the good you want, but keep quiet about it. *Use periods of delay as a time of preparation.* When you have done sufficient inner work, the outer results will come. When the time was right, with one bold stroke Joshua took possession of the Promised Land quickly. You can, too!

THE RICH REWARDS AND HOW TO CLAIM THEM

After crossing over into the Promised Land, Joshua did not forget the prosperous-minded Caleb who had been his friend for more than forty years. Instead, he rewarded the courageous Caleb by granting him the first assignment of land: the rich vineyard hill country of Hebron, filled with springs, water and overflowing with abundance. (Joshua 15:13) The word "Hebron" means "friendship" and this rich gift reflected friendship at its best!

Was Joshua personally rewarded for faithfully practicing the Prosperity Law of Mental Acceptance over such a long period? Indeed he was. Not only did he become the first commanding general of the Hebrews, and their revered leader in the prosperous Land of Canaan, but he also received an entire city as a gift in appreciation for his leadership and accomplishments. He was given Timnathserah in the mountains of Ephraim located in the territory of Judah. (Joshua 19:50) This area, which became the wandering Joshua's permanent home, had prosperous significance. The word "Timnath-serah" means "fruitful, productive, multiplying." The word "Ephraim" means "doubly

fruitful" and the word "Judah" means "praise, accumulation, increase."

As you, too, use the Prosperity Law of Mental Acceptance in the various ways that are described in this chapter,
it can lead you into a more productive way of life; one that
is doubly fruitful, filled with praise, the accumulation of
good, and constant increase; one that can help you end a
restless search and settle down in a realm of permanent
abundance!

In preparation for these blessings of increase, you will
enjoy meditating upon and declaring often these words:

*"I take only the good from each experience. I let the rest
go. I am not hypnotized by present circumstances, events or
situations. They, too, shall pass. I begin now to recognize a
better set of circumstances as possible for me. My progress is
swift and joyous. Yes, I mentally accept and claim my
highest good now. Lord, I am ready."*

SUMMARY

1. Psychologists say that you can have anything that you can mentally accept, but that you must mentally accept it first. If you cannot mentally accept it, you do not get your desired good no matter what else you do.

2. Upon learning of the power of thought as a means of attaining one's goals in life, people sometimes rush forth trying to bring to pass that which they have not mentally accepted. Even if they get what they want temporarily, they do not keep it because they have not first developed a mental acceptance of it.

3. Perhaps this is why we learn from the millionaires of the Bible that *lasting success is a progressive process;* it does not usually come in a flash flood of overnight wealth.

4. Joshua gave the formula for invoking the Prosperity Law of Mental Acceptance in the Book of Numbers. The word "numbers" means "in the wilderness." It is during your wilderness periods that you will most need to use this success law.

5. Soon after Joshua had been freed from Egyptian bondage and early in his wilderness wanderings, he was one of the twelve spies commanded by Moses to slip into the Promised Land, investigate its conditions and bring back a report.

6. One reason the spies were sent into the Promised Land was to help them mentally accept the vast abundance and great blessings that awaited them there. Yet when they returned, the spies gave conflicting reports. Joshua and Caleb were the only two spies who were ready to claim the Promised Land.

7. The word "Caleb" means "bold and fearless." He described Canaan as a rich country, and he even brought back an abundance of fruit from the valley of Eshcol as proof. The word "Eshcol" symbolizes "great fruitfulness" or "abundant possibilities." Joshua was of the tribe of Ephraim which means "doubly fruitful." Caleb was of the tribe of Judah which symbolizes "increase and accumulation through praise."

8. Historians state that the Hebrews actually sat and wept all night over their plight—though their rich Promised Land was in plain view. It is a pathetic example of people rejecting their good.

9. Those who are successful in the use of the Prosperity Law of Mental Acceptance are those who: (1) dare to release the past through the practice of release, forgiveness, and forming inner and outer vacuums in one's life, (2) then mentally accept the possibility of something better for themselves. Those who hang on to the past, and reject their longed-for good never get it.

10. That which you hold on to keeps you in the wilderness. When you reach the point where you take only the good from each experience and let the rest go, your progress will be swift and certain.

11. The way to mentally accept your good is to change your point of view: Recognize another set of circumstances as possible for you. Then dwell upon those possibilities constantly. But keep quiet about what you are picturing.

12. Joshua used the forty-year period of delay in the wilderness as a time of preparation and planning. He turned this delay into a blessing. When you have done sufficient work inwardly, the outer results will come. The rewards to Joshua were boundless. As you use the Prosperity Law of Mental Acceptance, it can help you end a restless search and settle down in the realm of permanent abundance, too.

THE PROSPERITY LAW OF ATTRACTION

— Chapter 3 —

An English professor once spoke of observing the Law of Attraction as it worked scholastically among his students. Two classes that he taught were filled with bright, well-adjusted, interested, cooperative students. They came to class on time, wrote excellent English themes, were well-mannered and appeared to be prosperous.

His other two classes contained students who were just the opposite:

They came to class late, unprepared and excuse-laden. They were uncooperative and unattentive. Their homework was ill-prepared and they displayed a complete lack of interest in, or understanding of, the class subject. Most of these students were unkept in appearance and missed about as many class periods as they attended.

This professor commented on how the Law of Attraction had worked at the unconscious level to mentally draw each type of student to his own peer group: "Birds of a feather flock together." That is the Law of Attraction. These students, who had been placed in a class group according to alphabetical classification only, proved it.

Here is the classic story that illustrates how the Law of Attraction works: Scientists experimented by placing a female moth in a certain enclosed area. They released a male moth a few miles away who, within a short time, had found his way to the first moth.

HOW THE LAW OF ATTRACTION WORKS

The Law of Attraction is one of the basic laws of the universe. You are constantly using it, whether you are aware of it or not. In fact, you cannot help but use the Law of Attraction. The word "attract" means "to draw." You are a magnetic field of mental influence. That about which you constantly think, you automatically pull, draw and attract to you. What you attract depends upon that which you *dwell* upon in your thoughts, words and actions.

You attract into your mind, body, business affairs, and human relationships that which you secretly harbor: that which you love, and that which you fear, resent, criticize or hate. You do not attract what you consciously want so much as what you subconsciously *are,* according to your dominant thoughts and feelings.

You attract the things to which you give a great deal of thought and feeling. If you give much thought to injustice, you attract unjust experiences to you. If you give much thought to financial strain and failure, you attract those experiences to you. If you think in a certain way, you attract to you people who think in that same way.

We often see the Law of Attraction at work in the business world as it works through ideas held in mind, which create an attracting or repelling mental atmosphere to which people unconsciously respond. A businessman who dwells upon the goodness of God in himself and others, and who thinks about and expects to be successful, will radiate an attractive mental influence which will draw success to him on all levels of his life. Emerson described such a person:

"Great hearts send forth steadily the secret forces that incessantly draw great events.[1]

Another man in the same business might dwell upon negative ideas. He might see only the problems and troubles of the world. He might hold only limited concepts of himself, his family, business associates, the economic scene, or world conditions. If so, he would set up a negative mental atmosphere which would repel customers, prosperity and success from him, no matter how hard he worked on the physical plane of life.

HOW JOSHUA USED THE LAW OF ATTRACTION TO ACHIEVE PROSPEROUS RESULTS

It is appropriate that the word "success," which appears only twice in the Bible, should be found both times in the

1. Ralph Waldo Emerson, *The Writings of Ralph Waldo Emerson* (New York, N.Y.: Random House, 1940).

Book of Joshua. From the life of Joshua we can learn much about the success power of the Law of Attraction, and how we can use it to prosper.

A study of his life shows that Joshua *should* have been the appointed one to take the Hebrews into the rich Land of Canaan. As outlined in Chapter 1, he was born in Egyptian bondage, served as a slave in Egypt, and fled with the Hebrews into the wilderness. There he spent forty years and was finally commissioned by Moses to achieve the challenging task of leading his kinsmen into the Land of Canaan.

As we have already learned, Joshua worked closely with Moses in the wilderness. He gained an understanding of the power of thought from the mystical Moses, who was a master psychologist and an illumined metaphysician. Moses had been instructed in the secret teaching of metaphysics at the court of Pharaoh. Moses had used mind power to achieve amazing results when he led the Hebrews out of bondage, fed them in the wilderness, and led them to the edge of the Promised Land. So as Moses' servant in the wilderness, Joshua had every opportunity to learn about the prospering power of the Law of Attraction. Because of the infallible working of the Law of Attraction, Joshua was the logical one to lead the Hebrews into the Promised Land, and to help them settle there.

What is the mysterious Law of Attraction which Joshua used to get the Hebrews into the Promised Land — that same attracting power which you and I can use to take us into our own "realm of substance," which is what the word "Canaan" means?

From the time Joshua had gotten out of Egyptian bondage, he had wanted to possess the Promised Land. But, as stated in Chapter 2, a number of the Hebrews could not mentally accept this possibility—even after Joshua returned as one of the spies who had investigated its wealth, and brought back prosperous evidence that it was a land flowing with milk and honey.

However, their doubts did not stop Joshua from continuing to dwell upon the Promised Land. Legend has it that Joshua would often go to the top of a high hill in the wilderness that overlooked the Promised Land and study how to enter it. He even worked out a master plan for success by which he could take the Hebrews into the Land of Canaan in just three short days. And his master plan worked! At the right time he did so, even though they had viewed it from afar for forty years and had considered its capture an impossible task.

Joshua invoked the Prosperity Law of Attraction in these ways:

a) By giving a great deal of thought to the Promised Land, and the possibility of entering it.

b) By studying the Promised Land, and picturing the successful possession of it.

c) By developing a master plan for the successful conquest of the Promised Land, then dwelling often often upon that plan. (His master plan is discussed in Chapter 4.)

d) By keeping quiet about what he was doing. Do not try to get others' approval of your master plan for success. Don't try to convince them that you are right. The doubts of others can dissipate your dreams. If you keep quiet about your dreams and keep believing in them, the same Power that gave you those dreams will give you all that is necessary for making them come true—at the right time, under the right circumstances.

As previously stated, you attract what you secretly harbor: what you love and what you hate. Joshua harbored his dream of getting into the Promised Land. He secretly loved that possibility. He gave it a great deal of thought. He planned how he could take it, and he dwelled upon his plan often. It was inevitable that in due time he would attract to him the Promised Land with its vast wealth.

It has been estimated that success may be the result of 98% mental preparation and 2% outer action. The way that Joshua miraculously crossed over the Jordan River in just three days, after having spent so many years in mental preparation, would give validity to that success estimate.

SHE LOST HER HOME THROUGH HATE

Yes, you attract to you that which you love, and that which you hate. Because this is true, you can never judge experiences that come to a person unless you know what he is secretly dwelling upon. People may appear to be very kind, positive and sincere. Yet if their lives do not reflect this, it is because they are talking one way, but thinking another. "By their fruits ye shall know them." (Matthew 7:16) They will reflect in their outer lives what they secretly harbor and dwell upon inwardly, rather than according to the "big front" they may show the world.

A chronically unhealthy woman constantly criticized a well-known public official in her town. She harbored a deep hatred for this man. One day she was informed by local authorities that her home would be purchased by the city and torn down to make way for a museum which would honor that very public official she had spent so many years hating! This woman unerringly proved that you attract to you that which you resent, criticize and hate.

SHE ATTRACTED THE PERSON SHE MOST HATED

Hate is one of the strongest forms of attraction. A businesswoman proved this. She had been involved with a married man. His sudden death left her filled with rage toward his wife, who naturally inherited his fortune.

As this businesswoman's hate grew, she attracted to her innumerable problems: ill health, indebtedness, and emotional turmoil. Ironically, the woman she hated most began shopping in the store where she worked, and seemed drawn to her department. The widow had known nothing of this woman's involvement with her late husband, and did not realize what she was asking emotionally, when she would approach the saleslady for advice about the purchase of certain costly items.

Frantically the salesperson asked, "Why is this happening to me? Haven't I been through enough?" She finally realized the irony of hate and its fantastic attracting power. It was only after she began to forgive and release past experiences and relationships that the rich widow faded out of her life. As she continued to cleanse her mind of negative emotions, she was able to resolve her own problems, and resume living a normal life.

HOW SHE ATTRACTED ALCOHOLICS

People who continue to have negative experiences unwittingly attract those experiences to them through their own negative thinking.

A widow of 75 ran a boarding house. She hated drinking. She considered it her duty to constantly dwell upon the evils of alcohol and to point out her beliefs to everyone she met. Yet she repeatedly attracted to her boarding house people who drank, and whom she had to evict. It was only after this vicious cycle had continued for some time that she sought metaphysical advice and realized that her own strong thoughts about drinking were the power that attracted problem drinkers into her home again and again. As she began to forgive and release her boarders, and refused to dwell any longer upon the subject of drinking, she started to attract the type of boarders she sincerely desired. She was freed of the emotional burden that attends hate, criticism and resentment. She began to feel freer and more at peace. Improved health and increased prosperity also came to her.

HOW SHE ATTRACTED BURNS ON HER HAND

A person's health often reflects the Law of Attraction. Another widow repeatedly condemned her daughter-in-law. One day she said to a friend, "Some of the things my daughter-in-law does just burn me up." Within twenty-four hours she had suffered severe burns on one hand and arm while preparing dinner!

She frantically telephoned a friend for prayer help. The friend candidly said, "That physical burn was attracted to you by a burning attitude. Is there some thing or someone that has 'burned you up' lately?" Aghast, the widow weakly replied, "Yes, my daughter-in-law." It was only as this widow stopped dwelling upon the actions of her daughter-in-law that her own peace of mind and health were restored.

The Law of Attraction might be described in this simple way:

The world you live in is the exact record of your thoughts. If you do not like the world you live in, then you do not like your thoughts.

An uplifted mind is a magnet for all good things of the universe to hasten to you. Whereas, a depressed, anxious, critical, resentful state of mind becomes a magnet for trouble to fly to you. The choice is up to you.

HOW NEGATIVE USE OF THE LAW OF ATTRACTION DESTROYED A MARRIAGE, GENERATED HEART TROUBLE AND PRODUCED TWO HATED BOSSES

There is a saying that "lightning always strikes twice." Don't you believe it! It is the Law of Attraction that can "strike twice" or many times. You attract what you love and what you fear—with lightening force.

A businessman's wife left him. His explanation was, "My wife left me for another man. It 'runs in the family.' My mother left my father for another man, and 'lightning always strikes twice.'"

The thing that had "run in the family" and had struck twice had been fear generated by the power of suggestion. Upon learning of the infallible Law of Attraction, which works through the power of suggestion, a young housewife exclaimed, "Now I know why our whole family has heart trouble—including our dog!"

Upon hearing about the Law of Attraction, a grandmother gasped, "Now I understand it. I always feared tuberculosis and cancer. The results were that my son got tuberculosis, and my husband died of cancer."

As Job discovered long ago about the Law of Attraction, the thing you fear comes upon you. Also the thing you repeatedly suggest to your thought and feeling nature comes upon you and happens. The results will be positive or negative according to what you have suggested.

A businessman had been successful over the years except with two bosses he had had, both named "Montgomery." He realized the irony of his situation when he learned of the Law of Attraction. He tried in every way he knew to get along with his present boss, the second Mr. Montgomery. He came to realize that the resentment he had felt for the first boss named "Montgomery" had doubtless attracted the second one to him. When he began to practice daily periods of forgiving the first Mr. Montgomery, the second one quickly faded out of his life, too.

HOW HE ATTRACTED ILL HEALTH, THEN DEATH

Another businessman said, "Everyone in our family develops high blood pressure and heart trouble by the time

they are 62 years old. They usually die by the time they are
65. I will, too, because it 'runs in the family.'"

True to his words, this man was informed by his physician
at the age of 62 that he had high blood pressure and heart
trouble. He immediately retired from his job to await the
worst. As he had expected, his health steadily declined.
Right on schedule, he passed on at the age of 65.

You attract in your health, financial affairs and in your
family relationships that which you secretly harbor: that
which you love, appreciate—and that which you hate, resent, criticize or fear.

HOW TO ATTRACT HAPPY RESULTS

In his book, *The Sunlit Way*[2], Dr. Ernest Wilson explained the Law of Attraction:

"There is always work for the right man, and at good
wages with even bigger opportunities ready when he has
proved himself capable and worthy. But even the right
man is no exception to the law of right thinking.

"A fearful mental attitude often keeps away from us
the good that God has for us . . . Fear and worry, the ad-
verse mental pictures that we established in mind, form
strong barriers against the good we desire . . . A resistant
mental attitude holds back the demonstration. When we
dissolve the barriers of repellent thought, and substitute a
receptive attitude, good things come to us in unexpected
and wonderful ways, and sometimes with a promptness
that is astonishing."

---

2. Unity Books, Unity Village, Mo., 64065.

Is there someone you are resisting and mentally fighting? Is there some condition in mind, body, financial affairs or human relationships you are mentally resenting? Your resistance is holding back your good.

How do you clear up mental resistance which has repelled the very blessings you so much desire?

What Not to Do: Stop picturing yourself as weak or misunderstood. Stop dramatizing yourself as a martyr. If you want to be thought of as long-suffering, you will always have something to suffer long about!

Do not take on the troubles of the world either. To do so only makes your life more complex and destroys your good. Withdraw your strong negative thoughts and feelings on all levels of life. Do not plan on trouble. Even if it temporarily appears, do not dwell on it or try to explain it. Let it go.

What to Do: Begin picturing anew the good you want. Practice quietly expecting it. Picture the best, not only for yourself, but also for others. Work out your own master plan for success. Then like Joshua on Mt. Nebo, quietly dwell upon it. As you do so daily, successful results will begin to appear.

HOW SHE ATTRACTED WEALTH AFTER HAVING EXPERIENCED POVERTY

A divorced woman had long dwelled upon the challenges that several unsuccessful marriages, and several problem children resulting from those marriages, had presented. For many years she had dramatized herself as a long-suffering martyr, and her problems had only multiplied. Her theme song had been, "Poor, unlucky me. What a hard life I have had. Everything happens to me."

True to her words, the Law of Attraction had consistently produced more hard times for her to face, in the form of ill health, family problems, indebtedness, even abject poverty. At the time this woman learned of the Law of Attraction, she was living from one day to the next, often wondering how she would meet the rent and provide food and clothing for her growing teenage children. She had difficulty keeping them in school and out of trouble. Along with job insecurity, there were painful health problems that had also defied solution.

As she began to study the Law of Attraction, she realized that she had become a martyr to her problems, and had intensely dramatized them from day to day. So she deliberately reversed her thoughts and her words. She began to praise and bless every sign of improvement in her health, children, job and financial affairs. She realized that *you cannot force your good but you can invite it by dwelling upon its possibilities.*

As she took time daily to think of all the good she would like to experience in her life, she reversed what she was attracting! A better job was offered her. One of her children entered the Armed Forces and began sending home a monthly allotment check. The other children improved their attitudes, behavior and school work. One child got a part-time job which helped to provide him with clothes and spending money.

As this woman's attitude became more positive, so did her health. One day she received a letter from an attorney in her home state, stating that a relative had passed away and left his *entire* estate to her. It consisted of a house, car, antique furniture, a mink coat, valuable jewelry and stocks. Her whole life soon reflected the blessings that this increased abundance made possible. She proved that when you change what you think, you change what you attract. She also proved that you cannot force your good into your life, but you can invite it by thinking about its possibilities. When you dare to do so, your good can appear, even in unprecedented ways.

People sometimes complain, "But if you only knew what kind of family I have, or the kind of people I have to work with." Even so, the Law of Attraction is immutable. It says, "Like attracts like." Yes, to change what you are thinking will change what you are attracting.

HOW SHE ATTRACTED A HAPPY MARRIAGE

People with problems often concentrate upon those problems, and then wonder why they cannot get rid of them. Change what you are dwelling upon and you will change what you are attracting into your life. When you start to expect the best, things will begin to consistently come your way without laborious struggle.

I suggest that you daily dwell upon some inspirational passage in the Bible. Dwell upon some constructive idea in a book, or upon an affirmative statement that uplifts you such as: *"Vast improvement comes quickly in every phase of my life now. Every day in every way, things are getting better and better for me now."* Spend some time each day inviting greater good into your life, and picture it as a completed result.

A widow, who had long wished to remarry, did so after she began to daily declare, *"I invite the powerful, loving action of God into my life now."* She met "Mr. Right" in a matter of weeks and married him in a matter of months!

HOW HE ATTRACTED HAPPINESS, PROSPERITY AND CONTENTMENT AFTER HAVING ATTRACTED TRAGEDY

A businessman from Ohio wrote:

"Having been a tool and machine designer most of my life and dealing in mathematics and cold facts, there is nothing of much use to me if it does not work. I have found and proven to myself that having unshakable faith, a definite purpose or desire, and the willingness to abide with these principles, plus the faith that God will work all things out for your good, are just as sound a formula as any mathematical, chemical or physical law. We do not stop to figure out why 2 plus 2 equals 4 every time we want to work a mathematical problem. We accept it with unmistakable faith. *We also have to accept the laws of life the same way.*

"Tragic experiences had brought me to my knees mentally, physically and financially before I was introduced to the power of prosperous thinking. I was made aware of this philosophy by the engineer who was in Dr. Ponder's first prosperity class in Alabama in 1958. He went from a million dollar construction job in Alabama to a fifteen million dollar construction job in Ohio—as a result of that prosperity class. He is the man who designed the Wheel of Fortune about which she writes in several of her books. He gave me a copy of her book, *The Dynamic Laws of Prosperity*, which described the results that came to those in that first prosperity class. He suggested that I, too, make a Wheel of Fortune.

"The results? I am now happier, more contented, independent, and prosperous than at any time in my life! Many things began to happen right out of the blue that I didn't believe were possible. Positions opened up at just the right time. Money began to flow my way. People became more helpful. Even parking spaces were made available when needed. Deliberately picturing the results one would like to experience in life is a success method that surely works! Picturing attracts one's good."

HOW A JOB, HOME, FURNITURE, BOAT, SPORTS CAR, AND FREEDOM FROM INDEBTEDNESS CAME TO HIM

A California businessman said, "I used the picturing method to attract the best job of my life."

A housewife from Pennsylvania said:

"I made my 'blueprint of destiny' and put it where I could look at it every day. My children joined me in this visual practice. We soon found the kind of house we needed for our family, and moved into it on a lease-purchase basis. When we looked at our 'blueprint' we realized that our new house looked just like the one we had been picturing. Our dream had come true.

"I then cut a picture out of a magazine and put it in my daughter's bedroom. While browsing in a furniture store, we spotted a charming bedroom set back in a corner that looked like the one from the magazine. My husband said, 'Let's buy it. At that low price, getting such nice furniture is like being given a present.' Since using pictures to obtain what we want, my health is also good again."

A California housewife wrote:

"My husband had started his own CPA practice and it was prospering, but our expenses and bills never allowed us to save any money or get ahead financially.

"After learning about the fantastic power of picturing, we made a Wheel of Fortune with pictures of the things my husband wanted. (I delayed making one since I had no definite idea of what I wanted.) He pictured a Porsche car, a house on the water, money, a sailboat, and the bills paid. We worked on this, along with writing up our goals, during the summer. Then we forgot about it in the midst of full, busy lives.

"Nevertheless, little by little all the things we had put on that Wheel of Fortune started coming to us, even though we had not looked at it for a long time:

"A grateful client leased a Porsche car for my husband at no cost to him. That same client gave him a sailboat and free dock space for it at the beach. We rented a house at the beach just across the street from the water. We paid off thousands of dollars of indebtedness."

HOW YOU CAN USE THE LAW OF ATTRACTION
AND PROSPER

Joshua's message to you in this chapter is this:

Do not spend your time merely hoping and wishing that everything will work out fine in your life. Be equally as willing to take both the inner and outer action needed to help it work out. Joshua did not merely hope the Hebrews would make it into the Promised Land, nor did he waste time fretting over their wilderness experiences.

Instead he ascended often to the top of Mount Nebo. There he deliberately studied the Promised Land. He worked out his master plan for success—a plan of action that he could implement at the opportune time. He was fully prepared to take action, and did so unhesitatingly when the appropriate moment arrived. All that he had planned for during forty years then began coming to pass in just three short days!

You may begin using the Law of Attraction in a prosperous way as you dwell often upon these statements:

"I withdraw my strong thoughts and feelings from negative appearances in every form. I do not dwell upon problems, my own or those of others. I do not try to explain them even if they temporarily appear. I let them go, and begin again by reflecting upon the lavish blessings that are my heritage. I invite greater good, even lavish abundance, into every phase of my life now. As I give it my attention, I attract it. In this expectancy, I rejoice and give thanks."

SUMMARY

1. The word "attract" means "to draw." You are a magnetic field of mental influence. What you constantly think about, and dwell upon in your thoughts, words and actions, you automatically pull, draw and attract to you.

2. You attract into your mind, body, and affairs that which you secretly harbor: that which you love, and that which you fear, resent, criticize or hate.

3. You do not attract what you consciously *want* so much as what you subconsciously *are*, according to your dominant thoughts and feelings.

4. You attract the things to which you give a great deal of thought and feeling.

5. The word "success" appears only twice in the Bible, both times in the Book of Joshua. From the life of Joshua we can learn much about the success power of the Law of Attraction.

6. Joshua gained an understanding of the power of thought from the mystical Moses, while studying with him in the wilderness. He observed Moses' use of mind power to achieve amazing results for the Hebrews.

7. After having spied on the rich Promised Land, Joshua had a forty-year wait in the wilderness. During this period, he invoked the Law of Attraction by studying the Promised Land, picturing the successful possession of it, by developing a master plan for taking it, and by keeping quiet about what he was doing.

8. An uplifted mind is a magnet for all good things of the universe to hasten to you. A depressed, resentful, critical state of mind is a magnet for attracting trouble. Hate is one of the strongest forms of attraction.

9. Stop picturing yourself as misunderstood or weak. Stop dramatizing your problems or those of the world. Instead, begin picturing the best for yourself and others. Work out your master plan for success and quietly dwell upon it. Successful results will come.

10. You cannot force your good but you can invite it by dwelling upon its possibilities. By doing this, Joshua was able to enter the Promised Land in just three short days — after forty years of waiting.

HOW TO ENTER YOUR PROMISED LAND OF LAVISH ABUNDANCE

— Chapter 4 —

At first glance, there was nothing spectacular about the Promised Land. Canaan covered only a small area: 150 miles in length and perhaps no more than 50 miles in width. Its chief commercial value was that it served as a passageway between the prosperous trade routes of Babylonia and Egypt. Yet a closer look reveals that Canaan was a land even richer than Egypt, the country from which the Hebrews had originally departed.

After having spent so many years trying to survive in a dry desert, the Israelites were especially impressed with the green fertile land of Canaan which was filled with water and plentiful crops. No irrigation was needed to produce corn, olives and grapes in abundance. It was an area of hills, valleys, gorges, terraces, mountains, flowing streams and lakes. It contained forests, deserts, jungles, lush gardens,

75

swamps, and fertile plains with rich, black earth. Canaan seemed very special, indeed, because it had been promised as a permanent abode to the Children of Israel, who were weary of their wilderness wanderings.

Over a long period of time, the Israelites had been psychologically prepared to expect the Promised Land to be one of lavish abundance. While they were still in the wilderness, Moses had described the wealth of Canaan to them in detail:

> "For Jehovah thy God bringeth thee into a good land, a land of brooks of water, of fountains and springs, flowing forth in valleys and hills; a land of wheat and barley, and vines and fig trees and pomegranates; a land of olive trees and honey; *a land wherein thou shalt eat bread without scarceness, thou shalt not lack anything in it;* a land whose stones are iron and out of whose hills thou mayest dig copper."
>
> (Deuteronomy 8:7-9)

Over and over Moses had predicted abundant wealth for the Israelites in the Promised Land:

> "And thou shalt eat and be full, and thou shalt bless Jehovah thy God for the good land which He hath given thee . . . But thou shalt remember Jehovah thy God, for it is He that giveth thee power to get wealth."
>
> (Deuteronomy 8:10, 18)

> ". . . the Lord thy God may bless thee in all that thou settest thine hand to in the land whither thou goest in to possess it."
>
> (Deuteronomy 23:20)

"And Jehovah will make thee plenteous for good in the fruit of thy body, and in the fruit of thy cattle, and in the fruit of thy ground, in the land which Jehovah sware unto thy fathers to give thee. Jehovah will open unto thee his good treasure the heavens, to give the rain of thy land in its season, and to bless all the work of thy hand; and thou shalt lend unto many nations, and thou shalt not borrow."

(Deuteronomy 28:11, 12)

The Book of Joshua is also filled with promises of the prosperity that would come to the Israelites, if they remained faithful to God. (Those promises are related later in this chapter.)

WHAT THE PROMISED LAND MEANS TO YOU

The Promised Land symbolizes the unlimited good which a rich, loving Father has for each person. This includes the unlimited abundance that He has for you! The Promised Land also symbolizes the unlimited good which every normal person desires. That good may not be spectacular. It may consist of the simple blessings of life: increased health, peace of mind, more harmonious relationships, financial security, more love, or a deeper understanding of the inner world of mind and spirit. *The milk and honey that had been promised the Hebrews in the Land of Canaan are symbolic of peace, prosperity and spirituality.* One's Promised Land might consist of a desire for something specific, even spectacular, too.

Like the Hebrews, you may have viewed your desired good from afar for a long time, but felt that you could not attain it. Joshua shows you how.

THE SUCCESS POWER OF PREPARATION

Joshua's mission had been two-fold:

1. To bring the Children of Israel into a realization of their inheritance of the Promised Land.
2. After they had been brought up into that understanding, he inspired them to courageously go forth and take possession of it.

However, preparation was first necessary. *Success finds the people who prepare for it.*

An inner realization of the abundance you desire always precedes its outer manifestation in your life, since the word "realization" means "completion." *Realization changes things. A realization of Truth will banish every problem.* Joshua first realized the wealth of the Promised Land when he, forty years earlier as a spy for Moses, had witnessed its abundance.

However, realization is an inner process of mental acceptance that must take place on both the conscious and subconscious levels of the mind before results can appear. This explains why your good does not usually appear as soon as you have become aware of its possibilities. A realization of that good may come to the conscious level of the mind in a flash, but its mental acceptance of the subconscious level of the mind usually comes degree by degree.

In order to substantiate his realization of the wealth he had found while spying in Canaan, Joshua spent much time during his wilderness period studying the Promised Land from atop Mount Nebo. There he developed his master plan to enter the Promised Land and take control of it.

During his wilderness period, Joshua wisely refused to be hypnotized by the walled cities and the hostile forces he knew were in the Promised Land. He realized that anything can be disposed of mentally, and that anything can be created mentally; that the outer world of circumstances shapes itself to the inner world of thought.

It is reassuring that Joshua developed this understanding during his years in the wilderness of Paran. Because the word "Paran" means "place of much searching" or "region of much digging." Your own search begins when you become convinced that abundant good is your heritage. A period of inner digging for that good occurs when you learn that dominion of your dreamed of Promised Land is, indeed, possible. What a thrilling realization that is!

It must have been difficult for Joshua to await the right time to claim that long Promised Land for the Hebrews, because he was inclined to be a man of action. But Joshua did not remain idle while he waited. He carefully prepared.

After such periods of searching, preparation and planning, you may have to wait for the right circumstances to unfold before you can claim your good. Those circumstances may come later than you feel you are ready for them. Yet they come under "divine timing" so that everyone involved is blessed and prospered. The important point is this:

Work out your master plan for success in detail, even while still in a wilderness period. Like Joshua, you will then enter your Promised Land at the right time. After complete preparation has been made within and without, it may happen quickly. One bold stroke and the Promised Land is yours.

HOW PREPARING, THEN WAITING, WORKED
FOR THE AUTHOR

In my own life, I have seen this happen. For a number of years, after I took up the study of the inner principles of success, there were definite improvements in my life, but the much greater success that I had envisioned did not come. As mentioned in my first book, *The Dynamic Laws of Prosperity* published in 1962, the power of prosperous thinking lifted me out of a poverty environment and set me on the road to my life work. But I knew that initial success was only a beginning. After the death of my husband in Texas in 1963, there were people there who bluntly said to me, "Why doesn't this excellent success philosophy that you teach work more for you? Why did you have to give up such a wonderful husband?"

I served a small ministry comprised of sincere people, but it did not grow or prosper for several years. It was during that apparently nonproductive period that I had to make the decision that I loved the inner laws of success so much that I would continue researching them and using them anyway—whether they seemed to "work" for me or not. That decision gave me a sense of peace and release, so that I relaxed and no longer strained to get results.

During that quiet period of almost a decade, I researched and wrote a number of books that became and are still popular best sellers, available now in paperback editions. Toward the end of that ten-year period, I moved on and established a much larger ministry elsewhere. I was soon able to enjoy my first home. Later, I made the long-desired move to Southern California, where my world has continued to expand and be enriched, both professionally and personally.

Like Joshua, when the wait was finally over, I was ready to move forward into what became my Promised Land. The tangible and intangible blessings I now enjoy made that long period of study, overcoming and preparation more than worth the effort.

THE FIRST STEP IN JOSHUA'S SUCCESS PLAN: ARISE, DO SOMETHING

That the word "Canaan" means "realm of substance" has great significance. Just as the Land of Canaan covered only a small geographical area, even a small degree of understanding on your part that substance is the key to all wealth can help you claim greater good in your life! The rich realm of universal substance releases its abundance to you in ways as simple as those used by Joshua to cross over the Jordan River and enter the Land of Canaan.

A famous sports figure has said, "To be successful, you've got to be goal-oriented." Joshua was a master strategist, a master planner. He knew that prosperity is a planned result and that unless there are plans, there can be no permanent results. Like Joshua, those who succeed after a long period of barren experiences are those who have quietly planned for that success "through thick and thin."

Joshua's master plan for success included four simple steps:

First. When Jehovah said, "Arise, go over this Jordan" Joshua was ready. (Joshua 1:2) Joshua then immediately went into the Hebrew camp and said, "Prepare, for within three days you are to pass over this Jordan, to go in and possess the land which Jehovah your God giveth you to possess." (Joshua 1:11)

The Jordan River symbolizes any barrier that stands between you and your desired good, but *often that barrier is much less difficult to penetrate than it looks.* For years the Hebrews had looked at their Promised Land across this river. They had said, "We would like to go in and possess it, but how can we get across the Jordan?"

The Jordan River wasn't very big. To an American or European the Jordan River would probably look like a large creek, but to these people who had been in the desert for so long, it looked like an extraordinary amount of water. To them, the Jordan River seemed like a tremendous barrier. Even though that barrier was mainly a psychological one, they had sat idly looking at it, regarding it as a tremendous challenge for many years. Yet Joshua suddenly appeared and said, "Prepare, for within three days we will cross over the Jordan and possess our Promised Land."

When Jehovah said to Joshua, "Arise," He meant "Rise up in your thinking. Do something to start moving toward your good, so that your good can start moving toward you.

When you dare to do so, your good will probably meet you more than half way."

JEHOVAH'S SUCCESS COMMANDS TO THE HEBREWS

Remember this: When you make the move forward in faith, as did the Israelites, you can do so with Jehovah's rich promises of success ringing in your ears:

"Every place that the sole of your foot shall tread upon, to you have I given it . . . There shall not any man be able to stand before thee all the days of thy life: as I was with Moses, so I will be with thee; I will not fail thee, nor forsake thee."

(Joshua 1:3, 5)

Jehovah had promised Joshua:

". . . Thou shalt cause this people to inherit the land which I sware unto their fathers to give them. Only be strong and very courageous, to observe to do according to all the law which Moses my servant commanded thee. Turn not from it to the right hand or to the left, that thou mayest have good success whithersoever thou goest. This book of the law shall not depart out of thy mouth, but thou shalt meditate thereon day and night, that thou mayest observe to do according to all that is written therein; for then thou shalt make thy way prosperous, and then thou shalt have good success . . . Be not affrighted, neither be thou dismayed: for Jehovah thy God is with thee whithersoever thou goest."

(Joshua 1:6-9)

How did the Israelites respond to these success commands? With enthusiasm!

"All that thou has commanded us we will do, and whithersoever thou sendest us we will go."

(Joshua 1:16)

In fact, the Israelites were so enthusiastic about these success commands that they proclaimed that all who did not adhere to them would be put to death — meaning that when we do not keep in close touch with the inner laws of success, continuing to fill our minds with them — the good we should have dies for lack of inner nourishment. Thus we should often review the rich promises that were made to the Israelites, since they apply to us as well.

HOW HE PAID OFF A HUGE INDEBTEDNESS AND BEGAN TO MAKE $200,000 A YEAR

Yes, if you want to experience greater prosperity, do something to move toward it: Buy a new pocketbook or wallet. If you want a better car, buy a new key chain. If you want better clothes, clean out the closet to make room for them. If you want a better house, get the one you have in order. Then praise and bless it. *Do something to start moving toward your desired goals, so that they can start moving toward you. The good you want wants you!*

A businessman in Wyoming decided to conduct a prosperity class for his business associates. Although his associates liked the prosperity ideas presented, their first reaction was, "Those are great ideas, but they won't work for me." His associates were filled with "It can't be done" or "It's too good to be true" attitudes.

Nevertheless, this businessman insisted that they begin to use the prosperity ideas that were presented. At the class meetings, he led them in declaring prosperity statements aloud together. He invited them to make private lists of both the tangible and intangible blessings they wanted to receive. He asked them to go home and do something to start moving toward their desired goals, such as releasing old possessions to make way for new ones. He suggested that they make Wheels of Fortune, picturing on them the increased health, wealth or happiness they desired.

As his students did these simple things, their methods worked. The prosperous results they obtained excited and delighted them. They were soon a group of transformed and prosperous individuals. But nothing had happened until they *did* something. And what they did was not complicated, but simple.

As for the businessman who conducted that prosperity class, he was able to reduce an enormous business indebtedness of $800,000 down to $126,000 within six months! As he continued to use the simple prosperity methods he had shared with his business associates, he was soon out of debt and making $200,000 a year!

HOW A WOMAN IN AUSTRALIA PROSPERED
HERSELF AND OTHERS

You must *arise* in your thinking and *do something*, if you want to pass over the barriers that have stood between you and your Promised Land.

A lady in Australia reported that after she began to speak forth prosperous words every day describing the good she wanted, her husband was able to add some needed rooms to their home; they also bought a beach house. After her sister made a Wheel of Fortune picturing world travel, she soon left on a trip around the world! A friend, who wrote out prosperity statements every day, quickly developed a larger financial income. When another friend spoke words for the perfect outcome of her shy, retiring daughter's life, the daughter surprised her by promptly getting engaged to a prominent young man whom the family loved.

WHY YOU MUST ARISE AND DO SOMETHING

Since the Hebrews had been promised the Land of Canaan as a gift, why did they have to put forth effort to claim it? For the same reason that you and I have to put forth effort.

Canaan symbolizes the rich inner realm of substance out of which all wealth flows, first as ideas, then as results. Why haven't more people become wealthy if they are surrounded by this lavish universal substance?

Because substance is passive. It waits for you to deliberately mold it and shape it through your prosperous thoughts, words and actions. In the very beginning man was given dominion over this visible world of lavish abundance, as well as over the invisible world of unlimited substance. But it is up to you to definitely claim it for your personal use.

The history of mankind's progress reveals *there is no gain except when we put forth effort*. The things we attain easily, we often do not fully appreciate. It can be "easy come, easy go."

If you wanted to become a successful musician, you would expect to apply considerable personal effort to learn the principles of music, wouldn't you? You would then perfect your music through practice, practice, practice. You would not expect your teacher to perform for you.

Once Joshua and his followers arose in their thinking and put forth effort, this stimulated them so that they knew what to do next. He told them to prepare, for within three days they were going in to possess the new land. When you arise in your thinking, then you should do something to prepare to possess your new good. Do not question *how* you are going to get it, just prepare. This will stimulate you mentally so that you will know what to do next.

THE SECOND STEP IN JOSHUA'S SUCCESS PLAN: USE YOUR "NO" AND "YES" MIND POWERS

Second: Joshua sent two spies into the Promised Land to study it. (Joshua 2) When the two spies arrived in the city of Jericho, which was located just inside the border of the Promised Land, they made a tremendous discovery:

The residents of Jericho had seen the smoke of the Hebrews' campfires across the river. They assumed there were millions of Hebrews ready to invade them, instead of only about forty thousand.[1] There was no reason for the Hebrews

---

1. As many as two million people may have gotten out of Egyptian bondage, but many of them died in the wilderness.

to have had fears about entering the Promised Land, because its residents feared the Hebrews. The Canaanites had already been psychologically defeated by their fears.

The two spies that Joshua sent to check on things symbolize your "no" and "yes" powers of the mind—denial and affirmation. Before attempting to enter your Promised Land, always send your "no" and "yes" powers before you to clear the way.

Use your "no" power to say, *"No. No. No. I do not fear this situation. No person, thing or event can keep from me that which the universe has for me now. My good cannot be withheld from me in this situation. My good cannot be taken from me in this situation. All obstacles and barriers to my good are now dissolved quickly and in peace."* By saying "no" to hostile appearances, they lose all power to hurt you. *When you no longer fear them, you can conquer them quickly.*

Use your "yes" power to say, *"Vast improvement comes quickly in this situation. I now enter my Promised Land where I belong, quickly and in peace."* When you affirm entrance into your good, this makes it firm, first in your thinking, then in your life. The situation changes as barriers crumble away. Yet it all began when you first changed your thoughts and words about it through use of your "no" and "yes" powers.

HOW A BUSINESSMAN OVERCAME STRONG BARRIERS AND ENTERED HIS PROMISED LAND

A businessman realized there was a barrier between him and his goal. Strong personalities were involved that dominated the situation. After trying to cope with them unsuccessfully, the businessman turned the matter loose. He stopped talking about the problem.

Instead, he began to privately speak forth words of denial and affirmation daily. His words of denial had been: *"Nothing can oppose my good. No one can oppose my good. My good cannot be withheld from me, or taken from me, in this situation now."* His affirmation had been: *"With God's help, I now accomplish great things with ease. My good now appears in this situation in God's own wonderful way."*

The personalities involved began changing for the better. When he no longer feared them, he was able to claim his good in the matter without resistance from anyone. It happened quickly and peacefully, but not until the "no" and "yes" powers of the mind had been used to do their perfect work for him on the inner level.

THE "NO" POWER SAVED HIM FROM BANKRUPTCY

Joshua may have learned about the "no" power of the mind while attending Moses' secret school of wisdom in the wilderness. That there is dissolving power in the word "no" was one of the great secret teachings of the past. Ancient philosophers taught that man could dissolve his hardest experiences or conditions by saying "no" to them.

What you keep quiet about, you are also saying "no" to. Students of the mind have often spoken forth affirmative words describing their good, yet did not manifest that good because they kept talking about their problems. They scared away the good they were affirming with their negative conversations as they kept criticizing and condemning.

If you have not experienced the blessings you feel you should have in your life, check your words. What have you been saying about yourself, other people, and the world in general? Your negative conversations may have scared away your good.

I once observed a businessman successfully weather a very bad period in his life by not talking about it. All of his friends thought he was affluent. He had long enjoyed a wealthy life style, but because of bad investments, he suddenly found himself on the brink of bankruptcy. Yet nobody knew it. He refused to talk about it. He refused to give his financial problems any power.

The result? He prayed his way through that trying period. He made a tremendous financial comeback as he courageously faced up to the situation with his daily use of "no" and "yes" prayer statements. This method worked so well that he was soon enjoying the affluence and abundance that his friends thought he had been enjoying all the time! How wise he had been to keep his mouth shut when the going got rough.

HE ATTRACTED A MILLIONAIRE INVESTOR THROUGH THE "YES" POWER

It has been estimated that spoken affirmations can speed up results as much as 80 percent. A California businessman related how spoken affirmations of prosperity helped him to attain a thriving business.

He and his business partner went into a new venture in the Los Angeles area, but it failed. Undaunted he began to declare daily, *"I love the highest and best in all people, and*

I now draw the highest, best, most prosperous-minded people to me."

After using these words, he felt strongly that he should go to Palm Springs for the weekend. That same weekend he met a millionaire who insisted that if this man would open a business in a beautiful, new, prestigious shopping center in Palm Springs, he was bound to prosper. He followed through on this fine advice, and his new business in America's foremost desert resort boomed from the start! It all began with his use of the "yes" power of the mind through declaring prosperous words.

THE THIRD STEP IN JOSHUA'S SUCCESS PLAN: PERFORM INNER AND OUTER CLEANSING

Third: the next step in Joshua's master plan for success was to cross the Jordan River. In preparation for this, Joshua told the people to "sanctify" themselves—meaning to cleanse themselves inwardly and outwardly—with the promise: "For tomorrow Jehovah will do wonders among you." (Joshua 3:5) He told the priests to go into the river and "stand still" in the water's edge, bearing the ark of the covenant. (Joshua 3:8) As they did so, the waters parted and the people passed over into the Promised Land.

When you reach that place where you know it is psychologically right to take action, you should do so—even though barriers still exist.

You can first "sanctify" yourself by cleansing yourself *inwardly* through the daily practice of forgiveness and release: *"I now fully and freely forgive and release everything and everybody, who needs it, of the past or present. I forgive and release everyone. I am free, and they are free, too. All things are cleared up between us now and forever.* "

A Florida businesswoman wrote:

"An inharmonious work situation has become friendly and comfortable since I have practiced releasing and forgiving those involved."

You can "sanctify" yourself *outwardly* by cleaning up and cleaning out unneeded possessions in your home or business, as well as by cleaning up and cleaning out unneeded relationships in your life — either those relationships that are questionable or those that you have simply outgrown.

A California businessman wrote:

"I have found that releasing the excess in my possessions has brought a release of excess weight in my body. As I have practiced cleaning up and cleaning out, getting things and relationships in order, a facial nerve problem from which I had suffered for years is now clearing up. Also, as I have practiced releasing and letting go people and possessions which I had so tightly held to in the past, the arthritis in my hands is beginning to subside. *The practice of release is bringing blessed relief in so many areas of my life.*"

THE FOURTH STEP IN JOSHUA'S SUCCESS PLAN: DISSOLVE BARRIERS WITH VICTORIOUS WORDS AND DIVINE PROMISES

Fourth: The next way you should take action toward crossing your Jordan River — even though barriers still exist — is this:

a) Send your "priests" (high-powered thoughts of victory, and your words of success) before you to stand facing that barrier.

b) Also, review the divine promises that assure you that successful results are your heritage by studying some of the great passages found in the Bible, or by reviewing such promises in an inspirational book. "And Joshua said unto the children of Israel, Come hither and hear the words of Jehovah your God." (Joshua 3:9)

c) Let your thoughts bear the "ark of the covenant" by dwelling upon the divine promise, "All things whatsoever the Father hath are mine." (John 16:15) As you dwell on this promise, it helps you to stand still mentally and to "keep your cool" emotionally, so that barriers dissolve. They do not part until you peacefully face them with your thoughts and words of victory.

Even though you would like for the waters to part before you, your act of faith comes first. When you go forward to meet the problem in faith, first it begins to change and move. Then it dissolves completely. First, it parts. Then it departs.

HOW HE WARDED OFF FINANCIAL RUIN, AND REGAINED HIS HEALTH AND FINANCIAL SUCCESS

A businessman was very disturbed. Everything was at a standstill financially. He had been unable to meet certain payments on land which he was buying. If the payments were not soon met, an entire shopping center, a jewelry store, and a ranch would be in financial jeopardy. The pressure of developing his business properties had led to his declining health. He wanted to lead a less demanding life.

He and his wife had often found affirmative statements and prosperous attitudes to be the answer to their business problems. They decided to:

a) "Stand still" in the face of these challenges by declaring, *"This need will be met in plenty of time, because God gives the increase. God prospers us now."*

b) Together they studied uplifting Bible promises and inspiring passages from self-help books on a daily basis.

c) They also kept quiet about their financial predicament, discussing it with no one.

As they practiced these methods for cleansing their minds of fear, and for standing firm in claiming their good, results came: Although there had been no financial activity for weeks, they soon received an income tax refund check amounting to several thousand dollars. Next, buyers appeared and bought a strip of business property that this couple had tried to sell for two years! The sale was quickly consummated at the highest price they had ever asked for that land. Other properties were soon leased by a business firm.

Within a short time several business deals had been completed and this financial obligation was met. They sold certain other properties and turned their financial affairs over to a business manager. This man chose to spend more time developing his ranch and regaining his health. Not only was he freed of the worry and financial strain of long standing, but their income became bigger than ever — after he and his wife stood still in the edge of the waters of financial difficulties, and faced their challenges with constructive attitudes and words.

THE FIFTH STEP IN JOSHUA'S SUCCESS PLAN: GIVE THANKS

Fifth: As the Hebrews passed through the Jordan River, Joshua instructed them to pick up twelve stones from the water — one for each tribe of Israel. After arriving on the edge of the Promised Land, they built an altar at Gilgal using the twelve stones as a memorial of thanksgiving to Jehovah for having divinely delivered Israel's twelve tribes. (Joshua 4:19-24) This altar was to stand through the centuries as an abiding witness of their divine deliverance and ultimate victory over impossible odds.

When you have passed through troubled waters and are on dry land again, always give thanks. Don't take the good you have gained for granted. Do something in an outer way to render appreciation to God for the divine protection and for the divine deliverance you have experienced.

A SPECIAL THANKSGIVING PROSPERITY FORMULA

The people of the Old Testament had a special thanksgiving formula that can prosper you. *In Biblical times, giving thanks was not done through mere lip service. It always took definite financial form.*

They felt that the act of thanksgiving protected their health, wealth, and happiness and made their good permanent. *Before* embarking on a journey, going into battle, or facing any challenging situation, they gave "faith offerings" to their priests and temples in the faith that their mission would be successful.

After returning from any challenging experience, they went directly to the priest or place of worship and gave a "thank offering" in appreciation for the blessing received, and in order to "seal" their good and make it lasting.

Giving was not only considered the *first* step in financial increase. It was the *last* step, too—the one that resulted in a permanent prosperity that would be divinely protected.

If you have been able to demonstrate greater good in your life, but couldn't hang on to it; or if you have had a hard time getting your prayers answered in the first place, this may be the reason. When was the last time you gave a "faith offering" in anticipation of answered prayer? When was the last time you gave a "thank offering" in appreciation for the blessings already received in order to "seal" that good and make it permanent?

Please note that these special offerings were bestowed over and above their regular tithes, which were given consistently and automatically. The people of Israel gave numerous other offerings, too, including a daily offering, both morning and evening; a sabbath or weekly offering; a monthly offering; special Passover offerings; first fruits offerings; meat, drink and sin offerings, etc. *The purpose of these numerous offerings was to keep them in touch with God as the source of their unlimited abundance, and to remind them that there was nothing automatic about the vast blessings they enjoyed.*

Did such lavish giving deplete them? On the contrary! History reveals that the more they gave, the more they prospered. They never complained about their vast giving. Instead, they gave graciously and with "holy joy." They could not outgive a rich, loving Father, and they knew it.

Joshua's act of giving thanks as soon as he led the Israelites across the Jordan River was a reminder of the success and abundance that lay before them if they would remember to put God first financially, and would look to Him for guidance and supply in the Promised Land. Joshua's act of giving thanks was also a reminder of the divine protection and deliverance the Israelites had already experienced.

This act of thanksgiving is an excellent prosperity method to employ when you are finishing up old experiences, and entering new ones.

THE PROSPERING POWER OF A "FAITH OFFERING"

A reader wrote from Michigan:

"On a day when I was financially destitute, without job or funds, I remembered having read of the Old Testament method of giving a 'faith offering' *before* one's prayers had been answered. In desperation, I decided to try it.

"On the same day that I put my 'faith offering' in the mail, friends dropped by for a visit. They intuitively sensed my situation and insisted upon giving me some money. The next morning another friend, with whom I had shared some prosperity books, came by and made me a gift of money. I have now applied for an interesting job and the prospects that I will get it are good. *I am praising God for plenty!*"

THE PROSPERING POWER OF A "THANK OFFERING"

A reader wrote from California:

"When faced with dire financial problems, I faithfully recited these statements of thanksgiving: *'I praise and give thanks for abundance. My gratitude is boundless.'* The results?

"Restitution of temporary losses in financial investments has been forthcoming by leaps and bounds. Forgotten returns have multiplied without interruption. I now have money left over at the end of the month to help pay for our daughter's college education. I have learned that there is prospering power and a divine protection in giving 'thank offerings' after one's prayers have been answered, and I have done so in grateful acknowledgement for this incredible turn of events."

HOW HER HOME LIFE, MARRIAGE, AND CAREER WERE VASTLY IMPROVED

The United States and Canada are considered two of the richest countries in the world today. They are also the only two countries in the world that observe an annual day of Thanksgiving. No wonder they are so prosperous!

That the act of thanksgiving has miracle power is related in the following letter from Canada:

"Wonderful things have happened in our lives since I started praising and giving thanks. Everything is falling into place, and better than we could have ever hoped for.

"Even our originally very confused and hopeless marriage situation has now reached a stage that allows both my husband and me to feel at peace and, most of all, to help our children grow up undisturbed by their parents' problems.

"And I have found my right job. This I have prayed about for two years. I am now beginning a very special teaching career that will allow me to use my talents the very best way, and to help many people. This is the work I was destined to do. *I cannot over-estimate the power of praise and thanksgiving to straighten out conditions and to make things right in one's life."*

THE BASIC SECRET FOR GETTING INTO YOUR PROMISED LAND

Here is the basic secret for getting into your Promised Land:

Don't just contemplate the inner laws of prosperity and success. Don't just read *about* them, but put them into practice. *Do* something.

Joshua proved that every obstacle moves from the path of the man who knows where he is going; that all the world is on the side of the man who has a plan for arising into his good, and then follows it.

You are like Joshua when you know the laws of prosperity and have the courage to act upon them. Joshua's mission was to lift up the thinking of the Hebrews, to assure them that "it could be done." After they had been brought up into that uplifted state of mind, they were able to go forth under divine direction to claim that which had long been theirs by divine right.

In fact, *when they acted upon their divine direction, it proved to be unbelievably easy for them to possess their Promised Land.* As you use Joshua's success formula found in this chapter, it will be unbelievably easy for you, too, to go forth and claim the good your heart desires. First comes the time of "inworking" or mental preparation. Then comes the time of "outworking" or action, which produces happy results.

THEIR IMMEDIATE REWARDS IN THE PROMISED LAND

Upon entering the Promised Land, the Hebrews' first reward was that they were no longer dependent upon mystical manna from heaven for their sustenance one day at a time. Instead, they now feasted on the abundance found in their new environment:

> "And the manna ceased on the morrow after they had eaten of the produce of the land; neither had the children of Israel manna any more; but they did eat of the fruit of the land of Canaan that year."
>
> (Joshua 5:12)

As promised in my book, *The Millionaire Moses,*[2] the same thing will happen to you as you move forward into your Promised Land. Old methods of supplying your needs one-day-at-a-time will pass away as more secure and permanent methods of prosperity open to you. Yet the earlier

---

2. Ponder (Marina del Rey, Calif., DeVorss & Co., 1977) Chapter 4, "How to Gather Your Prosperous Manna."

"manna from heaven" methods of supply gave your prosperity consciousness a strong, inner foundation that will serve you well for the rest of your life. Because of having lived in that one-day-at-a-time prosperity consciousness — often provided in mystical ways — you will never again fear lack!

Upon entering the Promised Land, Joshua's immediate reward was one of freedom from the shackles and limitations of the past, as shown in the divine command to him:

> "Put off thy shoe from off thy foot, for the place whereon thou standest is holy. And Joshua did so."
>
> (Joshua 5:15)

The feet symbolize one's understanding. They also symbolize one's first physical contact with the visible world. Now that he had entered his Promised Land of abundance, Joshua was commanded to let go of limited ideas, memories, and beliefs from the past — especially those having to do with the visible and financial world. "And Joshua did so" gladly. As you follow the steps outlined in this chapter for entering your Promised Land, you, too, will enjoy the immediate rewards that were bestowed upon Joshua and the Israelites.

You will also enjoy declaring often: *"The walls of lack and delay have crumbled away. I now enter my promised land where I belong. I maintain it permanently, prosperously and in peace."*

SUMMARY

1. The Promised Land symbolizes the unlimited good that a rich, loving Father has for every person, including you.

2. Joshua's mission had been two-fold: To help the Children of Israel realize the Promised Land was their inheritance, and to inspire them to courageously take possession of it. His had been a prosperity mission of unlimited proportions.

3. But first preparation was necessary. Success finds people who prepare for it.

4. The word "realization" means "completion." Realization changes things. A realization of Truth will banish every ill.

5. Joshua had realized the wealth of the Promised Land when on his spy mission into it forty years earlier. Then came a long period of preparation, planning, and waiting. After preparation and planning, don't miss your good by not waiting. Under "divine timing" your good will come.

6. The steps in Joshua's plan for taking the Promised Land were:

   a) Arise, do something.

   b) Use your "no" and "yes" powers of the mind.

   c) Perform inner and outer cleansing.

   d) Dissolve barriers with victorious words, and by reviewing divine promises.

   e) Give thanks in words and financially.

7. When you have passed through troubled waters and are
    on dry land again, always give thanks. In Biblical
    times, giving thanks always took financial form: *Before*
    facing any challenging situation, they gave a "faith
    offering." *After* returning, they gave a "thank offering"
    in appreciation. The purpose of these numerous offer-
    ings was to remind them there was nothing automatic
    about the vast blessings they enjoyed; that God was the
    source of their supply.

8. The act of thanksgiving is an excellent method to em-
    ploy when you are finishing up old experiences and en-
    tering new ones. True thanksgiving always includes
    financial giving.

9. Under Joshua's leadership, when the Hebrews acted
    upon their divine direction, it proved to be unbeliev-
    ably easy for them to possess their Promised Land.

10. For this purpose you will enjoy declaring often: *"The
    walls of lack and delay have crumbled away. I now
    enter my Promised Land where I belong. I maintain it
    permanently, prosperously and in peace."*

HOW TO CLAIM YOUR PROSPEROUS JERICHO

— Chapter 5 —

Upon their arrival in the Promised Land, the first task the Hebrews faced was to capture the thriving city of Jericho —a green oasis of abundance, and a verdant patch upon the barren plain and wilderness of Judea. As the gateway to the land of Canaan, Jericho was very important to the Hebrews. It was the oldest city in Canaan, and the prosperous trading center for the entire Promised Land. The area immediately surrounding Jericho was rich and fertile, and prosperous trade routes led out from it in all directions.

What is termed "impossible" is supposed to be that which is "not capable of being done, or happening." To conquer Jericho seemed an "impossible" task for the Hebrews because, as a desert people, they had no implements of war. They appeared utterly defenseless from a human stand-

point. There was no logical way they could take the prosperous, walled city of Jericho.

Their task looked even more impossible because at the
time Joshua and his army went in to possess it, the people of
the Promised Land lived in two ways:

a) In little kingdoms of their own inside walled cities.
   This protected them from enemy forces.

b) Other tribes lived together in the surrounding countryside, caring for their flocks and herds in the hills
   and valleys.

Joshua knew that the Hebrews would have to deal with all
these enemy tribes, both in the walled cities and in the surrounding countryside.

HOW TO MEET AN "IMPOSSIBLE" SITUATION
SUCCESSFULLY

At this point Joshua did not know *how* they were going to
seize Jericho, so he first became quiet, prayed and meditated, in order to achieve an uplifted state of mind. He did
not rush in and try to force a result.

In a quiet state of mind, Joshua realized that the Hebrews
were fearful, and that their fear had to be dissolved before
they could conquer Jericho. To neutralize this fear, he
asked that all the people who had grown up in the desert be
circumcized. The word "circumcize" means "to cut off."
The spiritual act of circumcision symbolized cutting off fear
among his followers.

Any time you are faced with an impossible situation, you

can use the "no" power of the mind to erase, cleanse, eliminate and cut off fear in your thinking. As mentioned in Chapter 4, the "no" attitude of mind has a dissolving power.

When you feel defenseless, do not rush about trying to meet the situation head on with some outer action. Become quiet, and work inwardly to attain an uplifted state of mind. Then observe circumcision by using your "no" power of the mind to cut off fear. When you no longer feel fearful, you are well on the way to achieving successful results in what you had thought was an "impossible" situation.

You can cut off fear with these thoughts: *"Nothing is impossible with God, so I do not accept this as an 'impossible' situation. With God's help, the impossible now comes to pass in this situation."*

After using your "no" power in this way, if you really believe that a change for the better is taking place, it will occur. You can count on it!

HOW THIS METHOD OVERCAME OBSTACLES FOR THE AUTHOR

When you overcome obstacles and enter new longed-for experiences, you have just entered your Promised Land. As the Hebrews discovered at Jericho, there are often those last enemy forces that have to be overcome after you get into your Promised Land, before you can fully possess it.

It happened to me when I entered the ministry. Even though I arrived at my first church with only $30 in my pocket and with my young son in tow, it was a dream come true to finally be entering a field of work I felt destined to follow. Yet upon assignment to that first church, two of the trustees objected. They argued that I was "too young" and had no experience. Nor were they happy about my being widowed with a lively young son. They would have preferred a minister with a more balanced family image.

Looking back, I can now sympathize with their logical objections. But at a time when it had already taken several major miracles to get me into a new field of work, their objections seemed merciless. I secretly felt they could hardly afford to be "nitpickers" because it was not a choice assignment.

Taking the job meant I would be working around the clock with practically no time of my own. There was no guaranteed income or vacation benefits. Getting sick was out of the question because there was not another qualified minister of our denomination in the state. The two objecting trustees were also reluctant to provide my son and me with one room in which to live.

Because that area of the country was not yet very receptive to the "new thought" message of Truth I would be teaching, I seemed destined to have only a small congregation, no matter how hard I worked. I *did* seem "young" when compared with the last several ministers — all of whom had been almost twice my age. However, each one of them had been an inexperienced, beginning minister, too. That church could not afford to employ a more experienced one then.

At the time, I would have appreciated more encouragement for taking a job that no one else wanted. I assured my critics that, although their objections might be valid ones, I had been assigned to that ministry, and with God's help would proceed accordingly.

Like the Hebrews at Jericho, I felt defenseless in facing

my critics because I had no implements of war. So I got quiet and began to declare these words daily: *"I am not defenseless, because God is my defense and my deliverance now. All obstacles and barriers to the supremacy of spirit are now dissolved in this situation, quickly and in peace. The divine plan now manifests for the good of all concerned."*

The first indication that my prayer was being answered came when a third member of the board of trustees secretly offered to join me in prayerfully declaring those words every day. Within a week, both of the objecting trustees had resigned with no pressure from anyone. They were quickly replaced with more supportive ones. From that point on, that ministry went forward and I happily served there for five busy, work-filled years.

Although they are now both deceased, I shall always bless those two critical trustees. The prayer work I did about them so long ago had a cumulative effect, and was destined to bring lasting blessings into my life in ways I could not have foreseen: When I left that church five years later, it was through marriage to one of the trustees who had replaced one of my two original critics. That trustee was named "Ponder" and as a result of our marriage, my second ministry took me into another part of the nation where I was to found several new churches. Although he passed on to an untimely death only two years after our marriage, I shall always proudly bear his name professionally.

Perhaps it is ironic that to date I am the only minister to have served that little church who went on to become a noted author, listed in *Who's Who*, who has also received an honorary doctoral degree. I considered these to be Promised Land "fringe benefits"—perhaps in compensation for he enormous amount of prayer work I did just to survive in hat, my first, ministry. In retrospect, I now consider that :xperience of so long ago to be a special tribute to, and 'eminder of, the "no" power of the mind, which we can all ise to meet challenging experiences victoriously.

HOW THEY USED THEIR "NO" POWER AND PERSISTED INTO SUCCESS

From Spain a housewife wrote:

"We sold everything in the USA and moved to Spain with our teenage children. My husband, a very fine artist, was trying desperately to make enough sales to keep us alive. For two years we lived on brown rice. Daily we persisted in using the power of prosperous thinking. We tithed whenever we received a check. We prayed daily for guidance and supply. We made a Wheel of Fortune, picturing prosperous results, and we wrote out daily lists of the blessings we felt should be ours by divine right. At times we wondered if we had made a mistake, but there was no money with which to return to the States.

"Then we learned we were to have another child. We knew we could not stay in the small flat we were occupying, and that we would need more money for living expenses. So we continued to say 'no' to the appearance of financial lack and limitation. Over and over we declared: *'Our lives cannot be limited. Our financial income cannot be limited. Christ in us now frees us from all financial limitation. We are prospered mentally and financially now.'*

"As we persisted in saying 'no' to limitation, everything changed. A friend, who had built an enormous villa, was returning to the United States. She asked us to stay in her villa for a nominal rent. She also bought paintings. It occurred to me to visit the Hilton Hotel again to see if they would give my husband a show. They would! A new shop had opened and they displayed my husband's painting with great pride. The owner became my husband's manager. Now the sales of my husband's paintings are nonstop! Mail orders are even arriving from the United States. This past month he won the honor of the title 'Commandeur' and received a Medaille de Vermeil at the Brussels Art Fair. We are glad we persisted in saying 'no' to financial lack."

HOW AN ALCOHOLIC MADE A COMEBACK

A businessman from California wrote:

"I have come a long way in the past five years, since I have been studying along the lines of prosperous thinking. I have held a job more than three years. I haven't touched alcohol but once during that time. It used to be Number One on my Hit Parade. I gave up smoking five years ago. I have had ten operations, two since I started back to work over three years ago, yet I used only one week's sick leave.

"After twenty-eight years and seven children, I have managed to survive the breakup of my marriage. I have increased control of my temper and I am learning to curtail expenses and handle my financial affairs more wisely. These may not seem great accomplishments to many people, but to one who has been there, they are. I am slowly gaining ground and on the way back up. How has this come about? I have persisted day in and day out in saying "no" to the mess I made of my life. Over and over

I have declared, *'No, I am not a failure. Anything in my life that needs to be changed can be changed, and is being changed now. Vast improvement comes quickly in every phase of my life now. Every day in every way, things are getting better and better for me. I praise my world now.'"*

HOW A SERVICEMAN TURNED HIS ASSIGNMENT INTO A GOOD ONE

A member of the United States Air Force stationed in the Aleutian Islands wrote:

"I became acquainted with the prosperous thinking philosophy in 1971 when I was stationed at Kelly Air Force Base in San Antonio, Texas. I had been told by a friend back home in Nebraska that I should attend the church in San Antonio where Catherine Ponder then served as minister, so I did.

"From my attendance at the first service, I hungered to learn more. I began reading inspirational books. Several months later, I returned to my permanent base in San Angelo, Texas but still managed to drive to San Antonio frequently for Dr. Ponder's inspirational services. Then I was transferred to the Aleutian Islands.

"This was considered by many to be an unhappy and desolate tour of duty. When I arrived on Shemya Island, an outpost far out in the Aleutian chain, between Alaska and Russia, I began to declare daily: *'This is not a bad assignment. This is not an unhappy assignment. Only good shall come from this assignment, both during my stay here and long afterwards.'*

"I also declared: *'Divine order is being established and maintained in my life and affairs now.'* I began to show

God I meant business by putting Him first financially and tithing from my gross income on a regular basis. *The results from this line of thought and action have been nothing less than phenomenal!*

"I was promoted and received a raise of $50 the first month. Promotions are nothing new, but this was based on test scores that are virtually impossible to pass the first time. Yet I passed them and became one of the few to be promoted to staff sergeant on the first try.

"As a result of these same test scores, I was just this month selected to receive a bonus known as 'superior performance pay' which results in an additional $30 a month for six months. I had hoped to eventually apply for a part-time job opening here on the base, but that turned out to be unnecessary. Instead, I was approached and told that the job as theater cashier was mine for the taking. I am now receiving an extra $150 to $200 a month from that part-time job which requires little time and effort.

"There have been lesser happenings: I have bowled for thirteen years and always hoped to win a trophy. My dad has one and so does my younger brother, but never me. I participated in a bowling league here a few months ago, and now have not one, but two bowling trophies! Another of my hobbies is photography. I decided to enter a picture in the base photo contest and got it in literally minutes before the contest closed. It won third place and another trophy has been added to my collection.

"These are the most recent results from saying 'no' to the thought of unhappiness, loneliness and desolation, and, instead, opening my mind to universal good — even way out here in the Aleutian Islands. I could list other blessings that have come to me as a result of this mental technique, such as receiving the gift of a new car, and an increase in dividends on the stocks I own.

"Since I began to practice the power of prosperous thinking, I am a much more positive person. I have more faith. When something comes up that I am not sure about, I give it to God and say, *'No, this is not a problem. Please put this in divine order.'* Everything always turns out for the best. This simple technique has revolutionized my life for good, and this is only the beginning!"

WHAT THEY DID IN THE FACE OF DANGER

The next thing Joshua had the Hebrews do, after their arrival in the Promised Land, was to observe a Passover and participate in other spiritual activities. This symbolized their going to work on the situation from an inner mental and spiritual standpoint. (Joshua 5:10) They had also observed this same success principle much earlier: After their dramatic escape from Egyptian bondage, and soon after their arrival in the majestic Sinai wilderness—where they were to look to God for guidance and supply for the next forty years—they had also observed a Passover. (Numbers 9:5)

Specifically, the Passover was a great thanksgiving festival commemorating their escape from Egyptian bondage. Since they knew about the miracle power of thanksgiving, this particular thanksgiving festival was now being celebrated just behind the front lines before their attack was made on Jericho. *In the face of danger, they remembered past victories, feasted, rejoiced, rendered Passover offerings to Jehovah, and gave thanks.*

THEIR STRANGE PLAN FOR VICTORY

An interesting thing happened after the fear had been cut off among the Hebrews: Joshua prayed for specific guidance and got it! Jehovah told him just how to take Jericho:

Accompanied by the ark of the covenant, seven priests were to go forth with their trumpets, and lead the men of war. Once a day for six days, the priests and men of war were to march around the walled city. That was all—just march around it. On the seventh day, after a march around the walls seven times, the priests would blow their trumpets. Only then were the men of war to shout with a mighty shout. This loud vibration would bring down the walls of Jericho.

At first glance, it sounded like foolish instructions and a strange plan for victory. However, the sacred ark, which accompanied them, was regarded as having magic powers. It also symbolized God's lavish promises to man that "all things whatsoever the Father hath are mine." (John 16:15) The ark's literal presence reminded them of this great promise and gave them the courage to surge forward.

Seven was considered a sacred number of special significance not only to the Hebrews, but to other Eastern people of their era, especially the prosperous Babylonians. And the power of the spoken word involved in these instructions denoted psychological warfare.

Before the Hebrews ever crossed the Jordan River, the people of Jericho had seen their campfires on the edge of the wilderness, and were already nervous. They assumed that unlimited hoards of Hebrews were about to invade them. When the Hebrews crossed the Jordan River, the people of Jericho had tightly locked their city gates thinking, "This is it. We will soon be invaded."

But a strange thing happened. Instead of rushing in to take Jericho upon their arrival in the Promised Land, the Hebrews set up camp and got quiet. For days they did nothing—or so it seemed to the anxious people of Jericho.

In reality the Hebrews were doing the most important things, the inner things that should always come first in meeting any challenge: They were busy (1) attending to circumcision (cutting off fear), and (2) observing Passover (working spiritually, giving thanks). Joshua was busy praying for guidance, and working things out inwardly.

When you work out an impossible situation from within, it may look for a time as though you are doing nothing. Your way of meeting a problem may appear strange to other people, but you should not let that bother you. Human opinion has no power for overcoming "impossible" situations, and should be ignored. Instead, this is the time to:

a) Get into an uplifted state of mind through the practice of prayer, meditation, declarations of Truth, and inspirational study.

b) Cut off fear through use of denials or the "no" power of the mind.

c) Relax and await specific guidance about what to do next.

When the Hebrews did nothing outwardly, the people of Jericho became jittery. They asked, "Why don't those Hebrews fight? Why don't they attack?"

You cannot resolve an "impossible" situation on a human level because you, too, have no implements of war, so why fight and be defeated? You can only meet it victoriously through inner psychological and spiritual methods.

HOW HE CHANGED JOBS AND TRIPLED HIS SALARY

A railroad engineer in Arizona wrote:

"I was a police patrolman on a salary of $9,200 per year. My wife was working as a telephone operator, but stopped to spend full time at home as a wife and mother. We were concerned about living on one salary because of rising costs, but both felt she had made the right decision. Since we had been studying the laws of prosperity for some time, we decided that we would trust them to take care of us financially.

"We began to daily declare: *'There is nothing to fear, because we are the rich children of a loving Father.'* I privately declared in my daily meditations: *'I am a child of the prosperous universe. I am a child of fortune.'* We continued the inspirational study of our prosperity books.

"Shortly after my wife stopped working, my uncle, who is a train engineer, told me of some positions that were open in his company. I applied and have been accepted for a train engineer's position. The wages will be three times my previous salary, plus many other benefits for my family and me. It pays to get quiet about one's problems, ask for guidance, and to think and pray along prosperous lines."

HOW A BUSINESS EXECUTIVE PROSPERED
HER COMPANY

A company president from Texas wrote:

"Every Monday morning we have a staff meeting to plan not only that day's work, but also what we want to accomplish for the week and month. We also cover training and problem-solving areas. A basic part of our Monday morning sessions is our beginning: a prayerful meditation. The theme is usually derived from our unstructured discussions of our thoughts and problems. This practice combines to strengthen us not only as individuals but as a unified, trusting, loving work unit.

"As president of my youthful, growing company, I wanted to set a precedent for such regular sessions, and for other impromptu sessions, too, throughout the work week. It has not only increased our financial consciousness, but our spiritual consciousness as well. This practice has also given us the additional strength needed to meet difficult experiences triumphantly."

HOW SHE LOST WEIGHT

A housewife from Arizona wrote:

"I have had a problem with compulsive over-eating for many years, and have felt hopelessly addicted to sugar and flour. I felt so defenseless because I had tried all the usual methods for losing weight.

"I knew it would take a miracle to have my obsession with food removed. I've been given that miracle! Now when I feel like eating something that I know is wrong for me, I declare this statement over and over: *'Of myself I cannot do it, but Jesus Christ can and is performing miracles in my mind, body and affairs now. I am every whit whole.'*

"I have lost weight for the first time, and this is only the beginning. That prayer statement also helped me to let go a resentment of longstanding that had aggravated my weight problem. I feel so relieved and free. To face one's problems with spiritual methods really works."

HOW HE GOT A BETTER JOB

A housewife from California wrote:

"When my husband came out of the Navy after twenty years of service, he was fearful that, at his age, he would not be able to get a good job. So he took the first job that was offered him, although it gave him no chance of advancement. When he began to study the power of prosperous thinking, he realized that he did not have to settle for such a limited way of life.

"He began to declare every day: *'There is nothing to fear. I am going out and get a job that will pay me what I'm worth, because I am a child of God and He loves me.'* He soon went to work as a pipefitter at the shipyards at a much better income and with far superior working conditions. He is also in familiar surroundings that are congenial with his Naval background."

THE ALL-CONQUERING POWER OF WORDS

Joshua followed what appeared to be utterly foolish guidance. He sent the priests and the men of war to march around the walls once a day for six days—with no implements of war!

When the people of Jericho saw the Hebrews on the march they thought, "At last those Hebrews are ready to fight. We are finally going to get some action." While awaiting attack, the people of Jericho approached the walls with their implements of war.

But when the Hebrews arrived, they marched straight toward the main gate. Suddenly they veered to the right and began parading slowly around the city walls. Still they did not fight. There was not a sound from them, not a word was spoken. The people of Jericho stood motionless, spellbound, fearful of this strange performance. It was a silent march. Not a single arrow was shot from the walls. After their silent march, the Hebrews turned their backs on Jericho and walked back to their camp.

The next day it happened all over again. The third, fourth, fifth, and sixth days, this strange activity reoccurred. The people of Jericho kept fretting, "Why don't they fight?" It was psychological warfare, a battle of nerves.

On the seventh day, something new happened. Again the marchers appeared and silently marched around the walls seven times. Suddenly the instructions came, "Shout, for the Lord has given you the city." (Joshua 6:16) The Hebrews "spoke the word" with a mighty shout. This vibration

started a rumble in the walls, which began to swing back
and forth, toppling to the ground.

The people of Israel were taught to attach the greatest
importance to the spoken word, especially when it was expressed in a solemn vow or through specific words expressed
with feeling. The belief in the power of the united shout was
an ancient belief that was native to the Hebrews.

HOW TO PROSPER THROUGH THE ATOMIC POWER
OF YOUR WORDS

*Your spiritual victories can be won by means that may
seem as utterly foolish and inadequate to human reason as
that of the Hebrews. No matter how impossible a situation
looks from a human standpoint, if you meet it by following
your inner promptings, you shall succeed!*

You may have to meet conditions in life that look as hard
to you as those walls of Jericho. If so, you cannot break them
down by human force no matter how hard you try. Yet they
will crumble away with little human effort when you do
inspirational study, pray for guidance, and follow through
on the ideas and opportunities that come.

When facing hard conditions, do the simple things that
worked for Joshua:

a) Keep *very* quiet about the problem, so that you do
not dissipate your power in a negative way. "Ye shall
not shout, neither shall any word proceed out of
your mouth, until the day I bid you shout." (Joshua
6:10)

b) Declare words of Truth with feeling. "Then shall ye
shout." (Joshua 6:10) Yes, be very quiet about the

problem, but very loud in describing and declaring the good you desire.

When you "speak the word" with feeling, you release an atomic power. One mighty shout may do it. One good session of "speaking the word" with feeling may do it. Or you may have to march around the situation more than once and keep declaring words of Truth, day in and day out, over a period of time. As in Joshua's case, you may find it wise to invite others of like mind to join you in confidentially declaring words of Truth in unison. You have the power to speak words of healing, abundance, harmony, joy, love, protection or peace which will produce good results for you and others in any situation.

It has been estimated that the spoken word can speed up results as much as 80 percent. Imagine what the *shouted* word of Truth can produce — or words of Truth released in song. This may be why people who attend church healing services often report they have been healed. A dynamic power is released in chants, shouts or through words that are sung with feeling. No wonder the Psalmist declared, "I will sing unto Jehovah because He hath dealt bountifully with me." (Psalms 13:6)

The average person utterly discounts the fantastic power of his words. Yet he is reaping the result of them in his life every day. *The Hebrews proved that when you speak forth good words, you set up an atomic vibration that will crumble a false situation, causing it to dissipate completely.* Too many people are still inclined to read *about* the power of words, yet do not bother to speak good words into expression on a regular, daily basis. By not doing so, they rob themselves of the bountiful benefits that could be theirs.

HOW THEY OBTAINED BOUNTIFUL RESULTS

A New York housewife wrote:

"Since I took up the practice of speaking prosperity decrees on a daily basis, my life has changed. It is blossoming with an abundance of blessings I never before dreamed possible!"

A businesswoman from California wrote:

"So many wonderful things have happened to my children and me since I've been using prosperity decrees every day. I now awake each morning excited and looking forward to life's surprises for the day."

A businesswoman from Hawaii reported:

"Since I have been repeating prosperity statements every day, the results have been amazing. Here is just one result: Last week I was forced to quit my job because we had only one car. Taking me to work interfered with my husband's job. At first I felt depressed about this change of events. Then I remembered the power of words and began to declare over and over: *Something good will come from this. Things are getting better and better for me now.*'

"With that thought in mind, my husband and I relaxed and went out dancing. That same evening we met a woman who gave me an excellent job, and I started the next day. My new work is located only two blocks from where we live, so there is no transportation problem. A better job and more money! It all happened so fast after I began declaring prosperity statements."

A businessman from Maine wrote:

"This morning I used the statement: *'Divine love prospers me now. Divine love, expressing through me, prospers everything and everybody now. Divine love, expressing through everything and everybody prospers me now.'*

"This afternoon I received a $401 monthly raise — effective last week! My wife and I now realize the power we can release by speaking forth prosperous words on a daily basis. We will never feel defenseless again."

Many a person has struggled needlessly for years with the problem of supply, when his spoken words of abundant increase would have quickly released the necessary funds to him. These people wisely proved it.

You, too, can prosper through the power of your words as you meditate upon and declare often these statements: *"I no longer struggle needlessly with the problem of supply. My deliberate spoken words of prosperity release the desired ideas, events, opportunities and funds to me. The prospering power of words enriches my life and financial affairs. The bounty of the universe flows to me now."*

HOW HER WORDS HELPED A RELATIVE
AT A DISTANCE

Every time you speak a word, you cause the atoms of your body to tremble and change place. You can also cause situations, events, circumstances and personalities outside yourself—even at long distances—to improve through your spoken words.

A teacher from Missouri wrote:

"*'The forces of good surround, protect and heal you,'* was the statement I used for my 86-year old aunt, who had been hospitalized with a bad hip. I declared these words for her morning, noon and night, and many times during the day. She has returned home, is walking without the use of her walker and feeling much better. This is especially remarkable because she lives alone.

"I have used a similar statement for myself: *'The forces of good surround, protect and prosper me.'* It brought an overflow of students in my creative writing classes, as well as numerous invitations to teach additional classes throughout our school district."

HOW PROSPERITY STATEMENTS SPOKEN IN A LOUD VOICE MANIFESTED A MUCH-NEEDED JOB

You can always meet impossible situations successfully when you speak words describing the good you wish to see released in the situation. In the face of hard conditions—like the Hebrews at the walls of Jericho—you will find it effective to speak words of Truth *loudly and with feeling*.

A businesswoman from Texas wrote:

"Since I have been speaking forth prosperity statements every day, how my prosperity has increased! I had been unemployed for almost a year, and I lacked a car to get to and from work. Since there was no public transportation in our neighborhood, finding suitable employment was quite a problem.

"Two weeks before Christmas, I was desperate for work of almost any kind. I decided that although the usual methods of speaking prosperity decrees had helped me greatly, I must get more emphatic if I wished to get a job. So on December 9th I walked through the house *loudly* decreeing that I would find suitable employment and that transportation would be provided. I refused to listen to my well-intentioned friends who kept saying that the unemployment rate was at an all-time high.

"I continued speaking my prosperity statements loudly and with feeling every day. Five days later I received a call from the employment office stating there was an opening at the Police Department only a few blocks from my house! I applied for the job, got it and love it. They graciously send a car to pick me up each morning and to deliver me home at the end of the day."

SHE HEARD THE WALLS OF JERICHO FALL DOWN

A housewife from New York wrote:

"Often when I feel defenseless in the face of negative experiences, I declare over and over the names, *Jesus Christ*' or '*Christ Jesus.*' I constantly use these names for guidance, protection and supply. It isn't so much that a miracle occurs right then, but I know that one is on its way. I can feel the ethers literally crack (not unlike the sound of the walls of Jericho falling down) when I use those two names. I can feel changes taking place. I can feel things moving toward me and away from me. After I have affirmed those sacred names, the very things I wanted have a way of manifesting at the right time.

"My new marriage, our business, and my in-laws have all responded. When my husband 'bosses' me around, it is offensive to me until I remember to declare that: *Jesus Christ is the head of this business and in absolute control.*' Then I calm down. I have used these two names to successfully resolve all types of problems. The other night my niece had an unexpected operation in the middle of the night. I almost panicked until I remembered to declare those two names. Then I relaxed. She is fine."

HOW TO TAKE A CURSE OFF YOUR PROBLEMS

Joshua had probably learned about the creative power of words when he studied at Moses' wisdom school in the wilderness. In any event, ancient philosophers taught that every word brings forth according to its kind. You can build up or you can tear down with your spoken words. This brings us to one last success technique connected with the victory at Jericho:

After Joshua took Jericho, he placed a curse upon the city, "Cursed be the man before Jehovah that riseth up and buildeth this City, Jericho." (Joshua 6:26) The old Jericho was never rebuilt; it is still in ruins. The new Jericho was placed on another site.

Why?

The people of the East respected a curse. "I know that he whom thou blessest is blessed, and he whom thou cursest is cursed." (Numbers 22:6) They placed so much emphasis on the power of negative words that no one dared to rebuild on the cursed site.

Is there something in your life that has defied solution? If so, you may have placed a curse upon it through your negative words.

We place a curse upon our health, financial affairs, or family relationships when we speak negative words about them. Then we are not able to bring forth good in them.

You can take the curse off your problems! Get quiet and stop feeding them the substance of your negative thoughts, feelings or words.

You may have placed a curse upon your good through criticism. Cease finding fault, even silently and in secret. Stop complaining, and put away sarcasm from your speech. Do not prophesy evil for yourself or for another. Refrain from accusing others of resentment, jealousy or spitefulness. Cease from pettiness in your thoughts, words and actions.

Stop calling attention to the faults and weaknesses of others. Do not call your children "bad" or members of your family "a failure." *Have a good word for yourself as well as for others, or keep quiet.*

Any word but a good word is a curse. You may have placed a curse upon your own life through your idle, negative statements aimed at other people. Since what you send out comes back multiplied, the curse you meant for others may have settled upon your own health, financial income or family relationships. The new good you desire for yourself or for others cannot come until you remove that curse by removing your negative words.

HOW TO REMOVE A CURSE FROM YOUR LIFE

Declare daily: *"There is no condemnation in me, for me or around about me. Jesus Christ now heals all critical states*

*of mind, and the results of all critical states of mind. I am
now free to claim my good and to share my good with
others."*

Earlier Jehovah had indicated to Moses that the curses
that had overshadowed the Hebrews during that period
could be removed when they "hearkened" to the voice of
Jehovah, following His guidance for them, and practicing
the success principles He had laid down for them. (Deuteronomy 28) (See chapter 9 of my book, *"The Millionaire
Moses.")* Later, the prophet Malachi was to remind the
handful of poverty-stricken Jews who returned from Baby-
lonian exile that they could remove the curse of poverty and
the other ills that plagued them, and that they could once
more claim God's unlimited blessings for them, when they
again put God first financially through tithing. (Malachi 3)

HOW TO REMOVE A CURSE FROM THE LIVES
OF OTHERS

Declare daily: *"I now pronounce you free from your own
negative thoughts, or from the negative thoughts of others.
There is no condemnation in you, for you or round about
you. Jesus Christ now heals all critical states of mind and the
results of all critical states of mind. You are now free to
claim your good and to share your good with others."*

HOW TO REMOVE A CURSE OTHERS MAY HAVE
PLACED UPON YOUR LIFE

Declare daily: *"All negative thoughts, words and actions
are now withdrawn from my life. The results of all nega-*

tive thoughts, words and actions, placed upon my life by others, are now withdrawn. I am free to claim my good and to share my good with others."

YOU CAN REMOVE A CURSE WITH A BLESSING

You can remove a curse by replacing it with a blessing. "Bless and curse not." (Romans 12:14) I once found myself held to a situation I felt I had outgrown. In spite of my earnest attempts to free myself from that experience through the use of spiritual methods, I remained locked into it.

One day in meditation it occurred to me how much I had silently condemned that situation. I recalled the sage advice, "Bless a thing and it will bless you, but if you curse a thing it will curse you. If you place your condemnation upon anything in life, it will strike back with its condemnation upon your life. The only way to get free is to bless and curse not."

From that day forward I withdrew my criticism and resentment from that situation. I blessed it over and over with the goodness of God. In a matter of weeks changes came, and in a matter of months I had been freed to move on to happier experiences elsewhere—but only after I blessed what I had previously condemned.

HOW SHE TURNED A DISAPPOINTMENT INTO A BLESSING

A Texas executive wrote:

"I was very depressed as a result of three major disappointments that came in quick succession. I affirmed that right action was taking place, and that every adversity carries with it the seed of a greater advantage. I kept declaring that my good was on the way, but there were no signs of it anywhere. Then I realized that I was still condemning those three disappointing experiences. When I withdrew my criticism from the three disappointments and the people involved, everything changed.

"The following week the way opened for me to go to Washington, D.C. on a much needed business trip. I visited in the House of Representatives and met with leaders of Congress. I accomplished the goals of my business trip, and was in the White House on the Friday before President Nixon's resignation. Since returning home I have been able to continue my work successfully. *Everything quickly improved when I stopped blaming and started blessing.*"

HOW HE REMOVED A CURSE AND PROSPERED

A businessman in the Southwest wrote:

"Ever since I began blessing my present employer, our working relationship has greatly improved. Since I have been blessing my job, I have been awarded a sizable 'cost of living' raise. The power of blessing has brought unexpected surprises. I received a letter last week inviting me to apply for a new position which would represent a rise of status within my profession and a substantial salary increase. I was recently hired to do some interesting part-time work for a leading educator. This will provide me with a new interest plus extra cash.

"The power of blessing has also brought my wife a very pleasant part-time job, and additional income. She recently received a gift of money that made it possible for her to buy a long-desired gold watch. This piece of jewelry will grow in value through the years. *To bless what we have previously condemned brings very rewarding results!*"

PROSPERITY AND FAME IN THE END

Although Joshua's men burned the city of Jericho, the silver, gold, and vessels of brass and of iron were placed in Jehovah's treasury. (Joshua 6:24) That which had spiritual value and prosperous significance was retained from this experience (You will find this happening in your own Jericho experiences.) Thus ends the battle which marked the initial entrance of the Hebrews into the Promised Land. "So Jehovah was with Joshua, and his fame was in all the land." (Joshua 6:27)

As you use Joshua's success methods described in this chapter, the impossible becomes possible, and you can go forth to claim your own prosperous Jericho. This victory will mark the initial entrance into your own Promised Land where, like the successful Joshua, your fame and prosperity will doubtless spread throughout the land!

SUMMARY

1. To conquer the thriving city of Jericho seemed an impossible task for the Hebrews, because they had no implements of war.

2. Since Joshua did not know *how* to take Jericho, he became quiet, prayed, meditated, and got into an uplifted state of mind.

3. The spiritual act of circumcision symbolizes cutting off fear. Joshua realized the Hebrews were fearful, so he asked them to be circumcized.

4. You can observe circumcision by using your "no" power of the mind to cut off fear. When you no longer feel fearful, you will be shown how to achieve successful results in what you had thought was an "impossible" situation.

5. Next, Joshua had the Hebrews observe a Passover. This symbolized their going to work on the situation from an inner mental and spiritual standpoint. In the face of danger, they remembered past victories, feasted, rejoiced, rendered offerings to Jehovah, and gave thanks.

6. Under divine instruction, the Hebrews quietly marched around the walled city of Jericho once a day for six days with no implements of war. They did nothing, or so it seemed, to the anxious people of Jericho. This was a period of psychological warfare.

7. On the seventh day the Hebrews "spoke the word" with a mighty shout which disintegrated the walls of Jericho. Your spiritual victories can be won by means that seem as foolish and inadequate from a human standpoint.

8. From Joshua's victory at Jericho, we learn we can overcome hard conditions by:

    a) Keeping very quiet about the problem.

    b) Declaring words of Truth with feeling, even loudly.

9. Many a person has struggled needlessly for years with problems of supply, when his spoken words of abundant increase would have quickly released the necessary funds to him.

10. After Joshua took Jericho he placed a curse upon the city. It was never rebuilt on that site. Any word but a good word is a curse. If there is something in your life that has defied solution, you may have placed a curse upon it through your words of condemnation. You can remove a curse by replacing it with a blessing.

11. Victory at Jericho established Joshua's fame throughout the land.

WHEN YOUR PROSPERITY IS WITHHELD

— Chapter 6 —

When your good is withheld in the form of increased health, prosperity or happiness, you are in for a shock! *You* — not someone else — are withholding it! Emerson explained, "It is impossible for a man to be cheated by anyone but himself."[1]

This prosperity secret is clearly taught in the seventh and eighth chapters of the Book of Joshua. One of the greatest victories of all times had just occurred. The Hebrews had taken the city of Jericho with no implements of war. They were so elated over that victory that they wanted to rush forth immediately and conquer the next town of Ai, located only a short distance away.

---

1. Ralph Waldo Emerson, *The Writings of Ralph Waldo Emerson* (New York, N.Y.: Random House, 1940).

Joshua sent a detachment of men up into the hills to scout the town of Ai. Upon their return, the soldiers reported that only a small number of people occupied the little hamlet and the Hebrews could easily take it.

As their commanding general, Joshua consented and the Israelites marched on Ai. Yet before sunset that day, they came rushing back with the enemy at their heels. Thirty-six of their men were dead. It was a crushing defeat — one that had appeared impossible. Still it had happened.

Joshua was so upset that he tore off his clothes, fell upon the ground and cried out for guidance. After their dramatic victory at Jericho, why had this happened?

The answer came quickly: One of Joshua's men had stolen rich treasures from the spoils of war gathered at Jericho. Because of this theft, the Hebrews had been punished with defeat.

Before his men had gone in to conquer Jericho, Joshua had reminded them of an ancient law: The spoils of war were considered a sacred offering to Jehovah, the same as a tithe. (Numbers 18:14) No one ever kept the spoils of war for personal gain. Joshua had carefully instructed the Hebrews before their victory at Jericho that they were to take nothing they found there: neither gold, silver, fine clothing or other riches. (Joshua 6:18,19) These belonged wholly to Jehovah and would become a part of His treasury.

When they attempted to take Ai, one man in Joshua's camp had disobeyed this ancient law. Achan took silver and gold, as well as an elegant robe of fine silk, and hid them in his tent. It is easy to understand Achan's attraction to the Babylonian-styled mantle, which would be similar in value to a garment fashioned in Paris today. That the people of

Jericho owned such fashionable garments indicates something of the commercial progress of that era.

A universal wisdom always knows when one of its laws has been misused. When the Hebrews tried to take the town of Ai, they had been defeated, even in the face of the most promising circumstances.

When Joshua prayed for guidance, Jehovah explained why they had been defeated: One among them had taken something that did not belong to him. Worse still, he had stolen "of the devoted thing" or spoils of war from Jehovah. "Every devoted thing is most holy unto Jehovah." (Leviticus 27:28) This was considered a more severe sin than to rob one's fellowman, and it was punishable by death. (Leviticus 27:29) Defeat at Ai had been the natural result. Jehovah promised that if Joshua would find the thief and punish him, their troubles would be over.

The thief was named "Achan" which means "troublesome." Achan symbolizes "covetousness" which always results in much trouble and sorrow to those who let it dominate their thoughts and actions.

THE BASIC LAW OF PROSPERITY

A woman of considerable wealth once told me, "I learned long ago when a problem arises that it is an indication I have not given enough. So I always ask, 'What can I give?' Then I get busy giving it. This simple method has led me from poverty to affluence."

Here is a lesson in the basic law of prosperity: *When your good is withheld from you, it is because like Achan, you are withholding something you should be giving.* By withholding, you have stopped up the channels through which more good can come to you. If you are withholding the tithe (of which the spoils of war were considered a part), then you are robbing God of His rightful portion of all that He has given you. From primitive times, it has been felt that *the tithe is not man's to withhold.* (Leviticus 27:32) To do so can bring a far worse reaction than robbing one's fellow man. As the name "Achan" implies, more trouble and sorrow will appear.

One of the most brilliant treatises ever written on this subject is Ralph Waldo Emerson's essay entitled *Compensation:*[2]

> "The thief steals from himself . . . A man pays dearly for a small frugality . . . Always pay; for first or last you must pay your entire debt . . . He is base — and that is the one base thing in the universe — to receive favors and render none . . . The benefit we receive must be rendered again, line for line, deed for deed, cent for cent to somebody . . . *Beware of too much good staying in your hand. It will fast corrupt. Pay it away quickly in some sort . . . Everything has its price, and if that price is not paid, not that thing but something else is obtained.* It is impossible to get anything without its price."

Any time your good seems to be withheld, read Emerson's fascinating essay on *Compensation* in its entirety.

WHAT TO DO WHEN THINGS GET TIGHT

There is a saying, "When things get tight, something has

---

2. *The Writings of Ralph Waldo Emerson* (New York, N.Y.: Random House, 1940).

to give." The prosperous Truth is, "When things get tight, *someone* has to give."

If things are tight in your life, then *you* are the "someone" who has to give! *Life is thrown out of balance when any person withholds that which belongs to the universe. People with problems are people who are out of balance with the universe. They need to give in order to restore balance and order in their minds, bodies, financial affairs and human relationships.*

HOW SHE WENT FROM A "FRIGHTFULLY TIGHT" TO A BOUNTIFUL CHRISTMAS SEASON

A career woman in Texas wrote:

"Although I kept affirming plenty, Christmas was looking frightfully tight. I realized my good had gotten jammed up and that I had to give to make way to receive. Through giving of my creative talents, I was able to produce some personalized Christmas gifts that were much appreciated. I also gave by helping serve Christmas dinner at the Salvation Army and passing out presents to the children there.

"How did my giving come back to me? Gifts from family and friends made my holiday a bountiful one. A special gift came through a telephone call from my minister. He asked me to become sponsor for the church's youth group beginning the first of the year. I welcome this new experience and the satisfaction it will bring in so many ways. Everything changed for the better after I got busy giving."

HE FOUND $11,000 AND RECEIVED A $3,000
CHECK THE SAME WEEK

A businessman in Illinois wrote:

"I needed an immediate $3,000 income so I began saying prosperity affirmations for it. However, nothing happened until I remembered that giving is the first step in receiving. I decided to give by cleaning out my clothes closet and dresser drawers. I passed along those unused items to charity.

"In the cleaning out process, I found a savings account book with a bank balance of $11,442.76, plus several years' interest! I had forgotten about that account because it had been a gift from my parents. On Saturday of that week, a check from one of my clients arrived for $3,100. *If you wish to be prospered, it surely pays to give—by passing on what you are not using.*"

THE HISTORY OF THIS ANCIENT PROSPERITY LAW

Jehovah's tithing instructions to the Children of Israel were very specific:

"All the tithe of the land, whether of the seed of the land, or of the fruit of the tree, is Jehovah's; it is holy unto Jehovah . . . And all the tithe of the herd or of the flock, whatsoever passeth under the rod, *the tenth shall be holy unto Jehovah.*"

(Leviticus 27:30,32)

"These are the statutes and the ordinances which ye shall observe to do in the land which Jehovah, the God of thy fathers, hath given thee to possess . . . Unto the place which Jehovah your God shall choose out of all your tribes, to put His name there, even unto His habitation shall ye seek, and thither thou shalt come, and thither ye shall bring your burnt offerings, and your sacrifices, and your tithes, and the heave-offering of your hand, and your vows, and your freewill offerings, and the firstlings of your herd and of your flocks; there ye shall eat before Jehovah your God, and *ye shall rejoice in all that you put your hand unto, ye and your households, wherein Jehovah thy God hath blessed thee.*"

(Deuteronomy 12:1,5,6,7)

Returning to God a tenth of one's income as a sacred tithe to His work was not a new teaching to the Hebrews. It was a reassertion of an ancient practice. The picture-writings of Egypt, the cuneiform tablets of Babylonia, the early writers of Greece and Rome all indicated that, long before Biblical times, tithing was a universal practice among civilized nations. *There has never been a nation, however remote or ancient, among whom the practice of tithing has not prevailed!*

Tithes were paid in Babylonia in 2000 B.C., before Abraham was born. During the first seventy-five years of his life spent in their thriving city of Ur, Abraham had observed the prospering power that tithing had had upon the wealthy, progressive Babylonians. He doubtless received specific instructions concerning the prospering power of tithing from the elegant High Priest, Melchizedek. After giving "a tenth of all" to Melchizedek (Genesis 14:20), Abraham received a promise of protection and prosperity from Jehovah fit for a millionaire, "Fear not. I am thy shield and thy exceeding great reward" (Genesis 15:1).

The prospering power that tithing has upon one's affairs was passed along by Abraham to his descendants. His grandson, Jacob, vowed, "Of all that thou shalt give me, I will surely give the tenth unto thee" (Genesis 28:22). This success covenant helped him to also become one of the Bible's early millionaires. (See my book, *The Millionaires of Genesis.*)

Moses was not only aware of the prospering power that tithing had had upon his kinsmen, Abraham and Jacob. He had also observed the prospering power that the practice of tithing had upon the Egyptians when he lived among them during the first forty years of his life. A double tithe, or two-tenths, was paid by the Egyptians to King Pharaoh, who supported the temples and priests. In return, Egypt was by far the wealthiest and most powerful nation of that era.

Joshua had also observed the prospering power that tithing had upon the affluent Egyptians during the first forty-five years of his life spent in Egypt. He later was among those who received specific tithing (and other financial) instructions from Moses in the wilderness. The Books of Deuteronomy, Numbers and Leviticus are filled to overflowing with those instructions.

Just as the Babylonians, Carthaginians, Greeks and Romans had dedicated a tenth of their income and the spoils of war to holy purposes, so did the people of Israel. It was prescribed by the law of Moses and instituted by Joshua, from the time of their settlement in the Promised Land.

HOW TITHING LAVISHLY PROSPERED THEM

The fascinating thing about the Hebrews' tithing practices is this:

Even though they gave much more than one-tenth (they gave three-tenths plus many other offerings, all of which totalled about one-fourth of their income)—they never complained about their giving. They never said it was burdensome or oppressive to give Jehovah so much. No request was ever made to lessen or repeal the tithe.

Instead, upon their arrival in the Promised Land and for many years thereafter, they gave generously. Their gifts were "laid in heaps" at the altar. (II Chronicles 31:6) The Israelites gave with a cheerful countenance and dedicated their tithes with gladness. A festival of thanksgiving often accompanied their giving. Their times of giving were times of holy joy. *They gave not the last and the least, but the first and the best, and their giving made them rich!*

Indeed, the more closely the tithing law was kept, the more prosperous the Hebrews grew. *Over and over, their payment of tithes and offerings brought peace and plenty.* Giving was also a method for getting their prayers answered. *Tithes were believed to purge one of sin, illness and even to deliver from death.* None appeared empty-handed before God. The importance of tithing is shown in the fact that the Jews were not allowed to eat or lodge with a non-tither. Regardless of social or economic strata, people of all classes paid their tithes gladly. From prince and nobleman to the humblest Israelite, they poured forth "a tenth of all" plus much more. Their resulting prosperity proved the adage, "you will never find a tither in the poorhouse."

WHAT ACHAN'S DEATH MEANS TO YOU

This is a giving universe, as evidenced by the ebb and flow of the tides, the seasons of the year, night following day, and the profuse abundance of Mother Nature. You cannot cheat this basic law of giving and receiving, which functions quietly throughout the universe. It works regardless of your misworking it. You can only cheat yourself out of much health, wealth and happiness if you foolishly try to bypass it.

It is frightening to realize what happened to Achan when he stole from the spoils of war meant for Jehovah's treasury. According to law, he and his entire family were stoned to death. Their herds, tents and all their possessions were destroyed.

The people in Joshua's camp witnessed a universal truth: *You cannot cheat God without cheating yourself. When you withhold from God's treasury, you kill out your own good.*

To make matters even worse, when you withhold—you have to give anyway—but to the negative experiences of life. Because this is a giving universe, you usually have to give many times the amount of your tithes for illness, accidents, family problems, financial and tax problems, loss, fire, theft, legal entanglements, and a thousand and one other ills.

HOW HER LACK OF GIVING AFFECTED HER HEALTH

A California housewife wrote:

"I felt that tithing was a good thing—for somebody else
—but that I could not afford it. I thought I should pay
my obligations to my creditors first. If any was left over,
then I could contribute to God's work. How many of us
make this foolish mistake.

"A friend finally explained the tithing law of prosperity
to me. She said that if we didn't give voluntarily to the
positive experiences of life, we would have to give invol-
untarily to the negative experiences of life. But give we
must, because it was the law of the universe.

"In reflecting upon my many problems over the years,
I realized how true that was. In recent months, I have
been forced to give large sums of money to the doctors
and hospitals. I am grateful for the help they gave me,
but enough is enough. If the shoe fits wear it. So I am
now tithing. *I have a sense of peace about my present
and future that I've never had before.*

"I had also thought it was wrong to expect any return
blessings from God if I gave to His causes. Now I realize
how wrong I was. The prophet Malachi promised unlimited prosperity and protection to those who tithed. (Malachi 3:10) *I now expect to prosper and be blessed,* just as
my tithes are blessing and prospering God's work."

HOW HER LACK OF GIVING CAUSED MANY PROBLEMS

When Achan stole from the sacred spoils of war that which belonged to Jehovah, not only was he stoned to death, but so was his family. Your giving, or lack of it, can have far reaching effects — not only upon you. It can also effect the success or failure of those around you.

A woman in Arizona wrote:

"Although I did other bill paying and shopping, I decided to put off mailing my Christmas tithe until free moments were longer and the post office lines were shorter.

"That weekend my daughter ended up in the hospital, causing us all kind of distress. Her doctor said there was nothing organically wrong, and she was finally released. I had not begrudged God the tithe, but I had begrudged the time needed to get the money in the mail to His work. From now on, God will get my tithes 'hot off the press.' I will no longer put Him off, thereby putting off my good, or the good of other people around me."

HOW ONE FAMILY WENT FROM FINANCIAL STRAIN TO MONEY LEFT OVER

The word "tithe" means "tenth." People of all great civilizations have felt that "ten" was "the magic number of increase," and have invoked it by tithing a tenth of all channels of income to their gods. In modern times, the magic number of increase still can be invoked through the act of consistently tithing a tenth of all one receives to God's work. A businessman in Wyoming wrote:

"I always thought I did not have enough money to go around, much less to give God His part, the tenth. But after hearing that the word "tithe" means "ten, the magic number of increase" — I decided to try the tithing law of prosperity.

"During my first six months of tithing, I received a raise in pay, my son's feet were straightened through a much-needed operation, and *I even had money left over.* There have been no arguments about money at our house since I began tithing because, for the first time, there has been plenty to go around. I have given God's work more in the last six months than I had previously contributed in my entire life, and my giving has made me feel so rich! I have just learned that I have another raise coming up. *Tithing is the answer to our economic ills, both individually and collectively.*"

UNEMPLOYED, RENT OVERDUE, BEHIND ON BANK NOTE, THEN SHE PROSPERED

If your income has been limited, you may have felt that you could not afford to give. However, that is the very time when you could not afford *not* to give God his tenth. The fact that you are in financial difficulties shows that you are bound by small, anxious thoughts which are closing off the channels to increased abundance.

Tithing helps you to loosen up so that you can receive. Many people hold themselves in financial bondage because they have not been able to loosen up. To tithe is to let go. To let go is to open up. To open up is to receive.

A Texas housewife wrote:

"There is a fantastic power in not withholding, but in tithing 10 percent of all one receives to God's work. I decided to try it when I was unemployed, the rent was overdue, a note at the bank was two months behind, and there were no groceries in the house for my two children.

"After I decided to put God first financially, a friend sent me $20 as a gift. I tithed $2 and spent the rest on groceries. The way soon opened for me to sell some unneeded furniture, which made it possible for me to pay all my debts. *As I continued to tithe, everything straightened out.* I am again employed and prosperous."

FROM NO PROSPECTS IN FIVE MONTHS TO TWO PROPERTY SALES

A California realtor wrote:

"I decided to find out if tithing really works. I had not had a sale in my real estate business in over five months. My bills were long overdue and I was in despair. Within a month from the time I mailed my first tithe check, I sold two properties and listed two more! During that first month of tithing, I also found help for a health problem that had bugged me for a long time. *I know that others can find the peace, joy and abundance that I have found through tithing. It works.*"

HOW SHE GOT OFF WELFARE

A businesswoman in Missouri wrote:

"I was on welfare when I learned that you can tithe your way to prosperity. That was the turning point in my life. I started tithing and got a part-time job in a jewelry store. As I continued to tithe, I was offered a free ride all the way home to Canada for Christmas. During the month of January when I was laid off from my job at the jewelry store, I continued to study the subject of tithing. February 1st, I was offered the best job of my life! Since then, I've had many prosperity demonstrations: the gift of clothes, a better place to live, and a new car. The man I thought I wanted to marry moved out of my life. I see now that he was not right for me. *My life has been put in order since I started putting God first financially.*"

HOW THEIR PROPERTY SOLD AFTER BEING ON
THE MARKET FOR FIVE YEARS

A married couple wrote from Colorado:

"*We have had so many prosperity demonstrations since we began to tithe.* The first one was the sale of some desert acreage we had been trying to sell for five years! It works to completely trust God with one's financial affairs by tithing."

FROM HUNGER TO $75,000 A YEAR

A housewife in Hawaii wrote:

"*I want to tell everyone with financial problems to tithe!* When my husband and I first learned of the prospering power of tithing, we didn't have enough to eat. Bills had piled up. In the face of this financial strain, we started tithing 10 percent of every cent we received.

"Fabulous things started to happen. My husband went into partnership with two other realtors. A piece of property sold that we owned, and had tried to sell for a long time. We stand to make $75,000 this year. We are now packing to leave for a vacation in Canada. *What a drastic change has come in our life style since we began to put God first financially. We are now convinced that tithing is the answer to all of life's problems.*"

HOW HIS DREAMS CAME TRUE WITHIN TWO YEARS

You can prove to your own satisfaction that your tithes will bring a greater increase than any other property that passes through your hands. Tithing is the best investment you can ever make because it puts you in touch with the ceaseless flow of universal supply. Every phase of your life begins to reflect that wealth.

A college professor in New York City wrote:

"Since beginning to tithe 10 percent of my gross income two years ago, so many of my dreams have come true: I obtained my master's degree. I moved from a $10,000 a year job to a $14,500 a year job. I now have a comfortable vacation home near the sea. Before tithing, I would not have dreamed I could ever have it. I have been busy running workshops and giving lectures, which has brought in extra income. A second car for my family has manifested. My wife and I are happier than ever in our marriage. We leave soon for a month's trip to Europe. After an estrangement of seventeen years, I have just experienced a peaceful, harmonious reunion with my father. *Since we began tithing, our every need has been supplied, and I now look forward to even bigger miracles!"*

HOW HIS TITHES QUICKLY RETURNED

You must take a stand for prosperity if you want prosperity to take a stand for you! To put your faith in God as the source of your supply, through returning a tenth of all you receive to Him, is to take that stand.

A California businessman wrote:

"The amount I have given in tithes has already come back to me. My tithes reappeared in my paycheck in the form of extra compensation for overtime. *It gives me a sense of security to realize that I cannot out-give God.*"

HOW HIS SALARY TRIPLED

A businessman in Arizona wrote:

"The one prosperity law which I had doubted the most — but which has proved to be the most profitable — has been that of tithing. I now have a new position at three times the income of my previous job!"

TELEPHONE RINGS WITH JOB OFFER WHILE WRITING OUT TITHE CHECK

A California businessman wrote:

"At the exact moment I was writing out a tithe check — I mean at the precise moment I wrote in a figure — the telephone rang! It was from an executive who wanted to know if I was available for a free-lance writing assignment. Was I! Having recently left a full-time job, this was the answer.

"I am happy that the timing with that tithe check was so apt. After leaving that full-time job, I had prayed that fear, doubt, worry and anxiety would be removed, both for myself and my wife. I knew that our supply was already there in the realm of rich, invisible substance, and that it would manifest as we exercised our faith. *That tithe check was the act of faith needed to bring immediate results.*"

HOW A 16-YEAR OLD GOT A JOB

A grandmother wrote from Florida:

"After my 16-year old granddaughter started tithing, she got a weekend job at the neighborhood hamburger stand. For a young girl with no experience, that job seems a miracle. She is thrilled and gives the tithing law of prosperity all the credit."

FROM NO CASH TO A $3,000 INCOME

A New York businessman wrote:

"I started tithing when I had no cash the first of the year. The steady growth of my prosperity has been amazing. July has been the biggest month to date, with over $3,000 received so far, and another week to go."

HOW THEIR INCOME TRIPLED IN EIGHTEEN MONTHS

A businessman in Virginia wrote:

"Since my wife and I started tithing from our gross incomes some eighteen months ago, our joint income has tripled! With God as our partner, we now have faith that our financial income will increase even more in the next eighteen months. It surely works when we get our human fears out of the way and trust God to prosper us."

HOW HIS INCOME INCREASED 8 1/2 TIMES IN
TWO YEARS

A Missouri businessman wrote:

"I started tithing regularly less than two years ago at a time when I felt I could not afford to tithe. Yet I knew a change had to come in my financial affairs; so I could not afford *not* to tithe.

"The results? Last month's tithe check was the largest to date! This month's will be even bigger. Today's tithe, less than two years after giving the first one, is exactly 8 1/2 times the first tithe. I am experiencing rapid and tremendous progress in my financial affairs. *I only wish I had opened the way for this to happen by tithing much sooner.*"

HOW HE WENT FROM NET TO GROSS TITHING

People often ask whether they should tithe from their net or gross income. The Israelites were instructed by Moses to give "a tenth of all" channels of income, which would be to tithe on one's gross income (before taxes or other deductions were withheld). Tithing on gross income was done under Joshua's leadership and throughout Bible times.

However, if you are just beginning to exercise your faith in the tithing law of prosperity, it may be easier to begin tithing from your net income. As the practice of tithing prospers you, you will grow into a prosperity consciousness where you will gladly and freely tithe of your gross income. As you continue to develop your prosperity consciousness, like the Hebrews of old you will probably go on to much larger giving beyond the tenth.

A Texas businessman wrote:

"I had been tithing net from one channel of income, and gross from another. Amazing things happened financially so that my checking account now reaches four figures at the beginning of each month. I have never had this much money in an account before. I have decided to tithe gross from all channels of my supply. *Peace of mind, as well as increased prosperity, have resulted from my practice of tithing.*"

HOW $4,448.61 CAME TO A HOUSEWIFE

A housewife in Oregon wrote:

"As a housewife, with no income of my own, I had always felt financially limited and frustrated. Since learning that a housewife can also tithe her way to prosperity, I have had wonderful prosperity demonstrations:

1. Received $400 income from babysitting in the last two months.

2. My husband received a 10 percent raise in pay.

3. I won $25 from a lottery ticket.

4. I inherited $4,448.61!

5. I have found pennies, dimes, loose change in our backyard, on the street and in parking lots — all tangible evidence of the universal substance that is available to us when we open our minds to it.

"It makes me feel rich to be giving so much through my tithes, and to be receiving so much in return. *I will never feel financially limited again.*"

HOW HE INHERITED $8,300

A West Coast businessman wrote:

"Besides the tremendous financial gains that tithing brought me, so many other wonderful things have happened. I gross $584 but only take home $398. When I started tithing gross, I knew I was going out on a limb. But I knew I had to do something in faith to increase my income, so I began to tithe anyway and did not try to reason through how it could prosper me.

"The first thing that happened was that *I had as much as ever to live on.* As I continued tithing, all heaven broke loose! I inherited $8,300 — which seemed a fortune to me. I was able to sell my old car and buy a new one.

"I wrote out a tithe check for 10 percent gross of my inheritance, my paycheck, and from the sale of my car. Before I could get that tithe check in the mail, I received another $110 unexpectedly. So I tore up the *first* tithe check and wrote a new one including 10 percent of the $100 just received. Before I could get that *second* tithe check in the mail, I heard from the Social Security Board saying they owed me some money. I finally made it to the mail box with my *third* tithe check. *Tithing is a terrific way to build your faith and prosper. I'll never count pennies with God again!*"

HOW HER SALARY WENT FROM $6,624 TO $11,616

A housewife in the Southwest wrote:

"After being in despair about our financial affairs for a long time, my husband and I finally arrived at the conclusion that the only thing left to try was to start tithing. We wrote out our tithe check and released it on a Wednesday.

"*Miracle #1:* We had applied for a bank loan of $5,500 to pay off debts. A month went by and we still had not obtained the loan. But only a week after we gave our first tithe, we got the $5,500 loan!

"Miracle #2: On the same day, my husband was able to secure an additional loan of $8,000 to buy cattle at only 8 percent interest. This was an extremely low interest rate at that time.

"Miracle #3: My husband had often asked the State for whom he works to let him furnish his own vehicle and receive mileage, but they had insisted that he drive a State car. After we began to tithe, they asked him to turn in his State car and furnish his own. This enables him to make a little off the mileage they pay. This was applied toward the purchase of a truck which he needed in his cattle business.

"Miracle #4: After buying the truck and the cattle, he needed a trailer to haul the cattle in. After praying about this, my husband was led to borrow a trailer from a friend, who was pleased he could use it. That same night, another friend offered my husband a demonstrator trailer to drive as advertising. My husband will receive a commission for every trailer sale he makes for this man.

"Miracle #5: Only yesterday I received word that I am getting a promotion which means my annual salary will go from $6,624 to $11,616! There are dozens of people on the staff well-qualified for that job, but the Lord chose to bless me with it. However, none of those well-qualified people are tithers, which makes the difference.

"Miracle #6: The things our children have seen and learned through our practice of tithing are things it takes most people a lifetime to realize. The miracle power of tithing will be invaluable to them for the rest of their lives. *If we could give a tithe check of $50 million, it would not be enough to equal what we have learned from the prosperity law of tithing. Its benefits to us have been unceasing."*

HOW TITHING HEALED HER OF A HEART CONDITION

One authority has estimated that 80 percent of the people who are patients in hospitals are there because they do not know how to give properly. *Man often blames his health problems on age, climate, heredity, when in reality it is the result of holding on to substance that he should be releasing in some form.* (No wonder the ancients believed that the act of tithing purged one of sin, illness, and even death.)

There is basically one problem in life: *congestion.* There is basically one solution: *circulation.* Congestion in the body, as well as in one's financial affairs, is often the result of a congested pocketbook. Tithing is an act of faith that brings about circulation and dissolves congestion.

A California businesswoman wrote:

"After reading about the power of making a Tithing Success Covenant in the book, *The Millionaires of Genesis,* I decided to try it. I wrote out in my Success Covenant that I would tithe 10 percent of my gross income first, before paying anything else. It worked! My expected income has been fine.

"*The surprise has been that tithing healed me.* I had had several heart failures and numerous acute health problems before tithing. My health is now so good that everyone calls me 'the miracle.' My employees and some of my friends are now making Tithing Success Covenants[3] as a result of what it has done for my health."

---

3. A free Success Covenant is available upon request by writing the author.

HOW TITHING SAVED THEIR MARRIAGE

You will find that putting God first financially, through the act of faithful tithing a tenth of all you receive, will straighten out and adjust every phase of your life.

Why?

When you tithe you are preserving your contact with God, the source of your health, wealth and happiness. This keeps you in touch with the unlimited blessings of the universe that are yours by divine right.

An Illinois housewife wrote:

> "My husband was ready to walk out on us because of financial problems. Thinking that I was going to have to face our desperate financial situation alone, I realized I needed God's help and started to consistently tithe.
>
> "That act of tithing proved to be an act of faith — the grain of mustard seed that was needed to move mountains. The first blessing to come was that my husband is still with us! We are slowly getting our financial affairs in order. Tithing has not only showed us the way. It has saved our marriage."

WHY TITHING SPELLS SUCCESS

With tears in her eyes, a California woman said to me, "Why didn't some minister teach me long ago about the problem-solving power of tithing? I can see that my lack of tithing has hindered my success. I have given 'love offerings' on a spasmodic basis to churches. I did not realize that I should consistently tithe if I wished to be consistently prospered and blessed. I can now see that tithing is orderly, scientific, and businesslike; that it opens the way for far greater results in one's life than the limited, spasmodic giving connected with voluntary offerings." After wiping the tears from her eyes, this woman gratefully wrote out her first tithe check.

Surely it is better to give meager "love offerings" and voluntary pledges to God's work, than to give nothing. Yet it is unfortunate that the voluntary offering plan has so often been emphasized as the only acceptable method of spiritual giving when, in fact, the voluntary offering plan has tended to unintentionally pauperize millions of people, as well as to pauperize their churches and ministers. It is true that the Hebrews gave offerings, but their offerings were generously and freely bestowed upon their priests and places of worship — only *after* they had given three-tenths (three tithes) of their gross income. Yes, their offerings were voluntarily given *over* and *above* their regular, required tithes.

If you are not satisfied with your spiritual growth or financial progress, this may be the reason. Check on your giving. Consistent tithing opens the way to a secure and permanent success. Spasmodic giving certainly may not.

WHERE YOU GIVE IS IMPORTANT

The Mosaic laws on tithing were very definite about *where* the tithe was to be given. The *first* tenth went to the priests and place of worship. This tithe was given impersonally. The giver had no say about how it was to be spent.

The *second* tithe was a festival tithe. The *third* tithe was a charity tithe.

If you are giving several-tenths of your income, rather than only one-tenth, then you may feel freer with your second or third tithe. But your first tithe should be given impersonally to God's work, or to people in God's work, with no stipulation of how it is to be spent by the recipient(s). Gifts, charities, obligations or upkeep of relatives are not a part of the first tithe.

Under the Mosaic law, the tithes were bountifully bestowed upon the priests of the Old Testament. The reason for this was that the priestly tribe of Levi did not receive any of the Promised Land during the reign of Joshua or later. Instead, Jehovah had specified to Moses that the priests were to receive *all* of the tithes from *all* of the Promised Land:

"Unto the children of Levi, I have given *all* the tithes in Israel for an inheritance."
(Numbers 18:21)

In turn, the priests gave "a tithe of the tithe" known as "a heave offering" to the tabernacle, temple or place of worship:

"When ye take of the children of Israel the tithe which I have given you from them for your inheritance, then ye shall offer up a heave offering of it for Jehovah, a tithe of the tithe."
(Numbers 18:26)

A good rule on giving seems to be to give at the point or points where you are receiving spiritual help and inspiration

—whether it be to the church(es) of your choice, or to a minister, inspired teacher, practitioner, or spiritual counselor.

You are not only enriched by your giving, but your tithes enrich the recipient so that that organization or individual is freed from financial strain. This enables them to fulfill their high mission of developing spiritually and of uplifting mankind, unhindered by material care—as were the affluent priests of Joshua's era.

HOW TO CLAIM YOUR TIDAL WAVE OF ABUNDANCE

The act of tithing has always been an act of spiritual worship. Tithing has always been a first requirement for spiritual growth among progressive civilizations and enlightened cultures.

As long as the Hebrews tithed, they prospered exceedingly. No other group of people has ever been able to exceed their wealth! But history reveals that long after Joshua's era, when the Israelites became lax in their giving, they came upon hard times and want. It was the wise prophet, Malachi, who finally reminded them they could again tithe their way to prosperity. (Malachi 3:7-12)

Your good need not be withheld! If your good has been withheld, check on your giving. Get busy giving in all the ways that are revealed to you. As you consistently invoke the ancient prosperity law of tithing, then make way for a tidal wave of abundance to reach you by declaring daily: *"Tithing spells success. I freely give my tenth to God, and I reap a hundredfold blessing. All that the Father has for me now comes to me speedily, richly, freely."*

HOW THE HEBREWS "SEALED" THIS VICTORY
AND MADE IT PERMANENT

Joshua followed Jehovah's advice and Achan and his family were disposed of for having withheld that which belonged to God's treasury. The Hebrews were then able to successfully capture the town of Ai.

In their hour of victory, the Hebrews followed their usual custom of gathering together in order to give thanks for having just been victorious in battle. (Joshua 8:30-35) Joshua built an altar unto Jehovah and the Hebrews displayed their gratitude by sharing with Jehovah their rich gifts of burnt offerings and peace offerings. In the presence of a vast assembly of "all of Israel" — which included the elders, officers, judges, priests, Levites, women, children, and even the sojourners — Joshua then read to them from the law of Moses.

These acts were a reminder that it was God who had given them the victory at Ai and had helped them to establish a foothold in the Promised Land. Through these acts of appreciation to God for His help, the Hebrews "sealed" their victory at Ai and made it permanent. Another reminder to us that *after* answered prayer, we should make it a point to give thanks — through our acts of prayer, inspirational study, and through our financial gifts to God. In these simple ways, we, too, can "seal" our victories and make them permanent.

A MEDITATION TO RELEASE YOUR PROSPERITY

"When my good has been withheld from me, it is because (like Achan), I am withholding something I should be giving. My life is thrown out of balance when I withhold that which belongs to the universe. I need to give in order to restore balance in my mind, body, financial affairs, and human relationships. I beware of too much good staying in my hand. I pay it away quickly in some form so that it will not fast corrupt. Everything has its price, and if that price is not paid, then not that thing but something else is obtained. It is impossible for me to be cheated by anyone but myself.

"The Hebrews gave not the last and the least, but the first and the best—and their giving made them rich. Over and over, their payment of tithes and offerings brought peace and plenty. Tithes were believed to purge one of sin, illness and even to deliver from death. It is still true today. Like Achan, I cannot cheat God without cheating myself. When I withhold from God's treasury, I kill out my own good. Furthermore, when I withhold, I have to give anyway—but to the negative experiences of life. Whereas, when I put God first financially through sharing of my consistent tithes to His work, everything straightens out, adjusts itself, and my life is put in order.

"Tithing is the best investment I can ever make because it puts me in touch with the ceaseless flow of universal supply. Every phase of my life reflects the wealth that tithing brings. It gives me a sense of security and joy to realize that I cannot outgive God! Because tithing is a terrific way to build my

faith and prosper, I'll never count pennies with God again.
Through my tithes and offerings to God's work, I now 'seal
my victories and make them permanent. I freely give m
tenth to God, and I reap a hundredfold blessing. All that th
Father has for me now comes to me speedily, richly an
freely. Tithing spells success and I prove it now."

A SPECIAL NOTE FROM THE AUTHOR

Through the generous outpouring of their tithes over
the years, the readers of my books have helped me to financially establish three new churches — the most recent being a
global ministry, *Unity Church Worldwide,* with headquar-
ters in Palm Desert, California. Many thanks for your help
in the past, and for all that you continue to share.

You are also invited to share your tithes with the
churches of your choice — especially those which teach the
truths stressed in this book. Such churches would include
the metaphysical churches of Unity, Religious Science,
Divine Science, Science of Mind and other related churches,
many of which are members of the International New
Thought Movement. (For a list of such churches write The
International New Thought Alliance, 5003 East Broad-
way Road, Mesa, Arizona 85206.) Your support of such
churches can help spread the prosperous Truth that mankind
is now seeking in the new age of metaphysical enlightenment.

SUMMARY

1. After one of the greatest victories of all times at Jericho, the Hebrews rushed forth to conquer the next town of Ai, only to be defeated.

2. This crushing defeat had seemed impossible, yet it had happened. When the distressed Joshua asked why, he discovered that one of his men, Achan, had stolen from the rich spoils of war gathered at Jericho.

3. According to ancient law, the spoils of war were considered a sacred offering to Jehovah, the same as a tithe. To keep a portion of the spoils of war for personal gain was punishable by death.

4. The word "Achan" means "troublesome." Achan symbolizes "covetousness" which always results in much trouble and sorrow to those who let it dominate their thoughts and actions.

5. When your good is withheld from you, it is because like Achan, you are withholding something you should be giving.

6. Just as the spoils of war in ancient times were considered a tithe which belonged wholly to Jehovah's treasury, so the tithe is not man's to withhold today. To withhold it can bring a far worse reaction than robbing one's fellow man.

7. Life is thrown out of balance when any person withholds that which belongs to the universe. People with problems are people who are out of balance with the universe. They need to give in order to restore balance and order in their minds, bodies, financial affairs and human relationships.

8. There has never been a nation, however remote or ancient, among whom the practice of tithing has not prevailed. The Hebrews gave not the last and the least, but the first and the best, and their giving made them rich.

9. Over and over their payment of tithes and offerings brought peace and plenty. Giving was also a method for getting their prayers answered. Tithes were believed to purge one of sin, illness, and even to deliver from death.

10. Achan's death is symbolic: You cannot cheat God without cheating yourself. When you withhold from God's treasury, you destroy your own good.

11. Putting God first financially, through the act of faithful tithing a tenth of all you receive, will straighten out and adjust every phase of your life. Tithing spells success.

12. The act of tithing has always been an act of spiritual worship. Tithing has always been a first requirement for spiritual growth among progressive civilizations and enlightened cultures. After Achan and his family were punished, the Hebrews were able to successfully capture the town of Ai. They "sealed" this victory and made it permanent through specific acts of thanksgiving. We should, too.

THE PROSPERING POWER OF MISTAKES

— Chapter 7 —

Many a success has been built upon an apparent failure. While taking possession of the Promised Land, Joshua proved this, and so can you!

The word "mistake" means "misunderstood," "to take wrongly," "to estimate incorrectly," or "a fault in interpretation." *Your mistakes are merely experiences which you have misunderstood!* You called them "mistakes" because you did not know how to interpret them correctly.

After entering the Promised Land, the first two towns that the Hebrews conquered were Jericho and Ai. The next town to be taken was the royal city of Gibeon. It was the chief city of the Canaanites, larger than Ai, and a stronghold in the Promised Land. (Joshua 9)

The people of Gibeon and several other neighboring cities had heard of the power of Joshua and his army: That they could break down walls without even touching them, as they had done in Jericho. The people of Gibeon were frightened by the powerful Hebrews, so they decided to outwit Joshua rather than fight his army.

As though they were people from a far country, the Gibeonites dressed themselves in muddy old clothes and worn sandals. This ragged, hungry group of people then appeared in Joshua's camp carrying patched water bags and stale bread. They were a pathetic sight.

Joshua was impressed when they explained that they had come from a far country to make a treaty with the powerful Hebrews. He felt sorry for these shabby strangers who only wanted peace. He honored their request and made a treaty with them, in which the people of Gibeon became allies with the Hebrews. In the treaty Joshua agreed that these people would never be killed by the Hebrews.

Very soon Joshua discovered his apparent mistake. Those ragged strangers were not from a far country. They were from the next town that had to be conquered — the town of Gibeon! Joshua had been deceived. Of course he was upset when he realized that he had been tricked. But he had made a treaty, and in those days, a treaty was considered sacred. The Hebrews were noted for keeping their word of honor. Once they gave their word about anything, they would not go back on it. Since Joshua had made a sacred pledge not to kill their people, he kept it even though they had tricked him.

THE WEALTH THAT CAME FROM HIS MISTAKE

But something good came from this apparent mistake. Even though Joshua seemed to have erred, he had not. The good that came from his blunder was this: The Hebrews went in and took the town of Gibeon, located in the heart of the Promised Land, without shedding a drop of blood or losing a single life. He punished the people of Gibeon for their trickery by making them servants of the Hebrews. They were never a free people, but their lives were spared. There had been no battle, violence or bloodshed.

Gibeon was a prosperous town worth saving because it opened the trade routes north and south into the entire Promised Land, as well as to surrounding countries. Joshua's apparent mistake proved not to be a bad bargain after all. A victory was quietly accomplished. Because of the thriving trade routes that were opened throughout the Promised Land, unprecedented prosperity was established for the Hebrews!

THE PROSPERITY LESSON WE LEARN FROM JOSHUA

From this episode in Joshua's life, we learn a great lesson: There are no mistakes. There are only experiences which we have not understood so we gave them a false interpretation. We labeled them evil when there was good in them.

Rename your "mistakes." Say to those apparent errors: *"Here is an experience that I have not understood, so I have labeled this experience incorrectly. I have falsely interpreted it by labeling it a 'mistake,' but there are no 'mistakes.' There are only experiences which I have not understood.*

"I rename this experience a 'success.' It is not a 'mistake.' Out of apparent failure comes success. Many a success has been built upon an apparent failure. What has appeared to be a failure can still lead me to success. Something good can still come from this experience, so I rename it a 'success.'"

HOW A MERCHANT PROSPERED FROM HIS MISTAKES

There once was a small town merchant who had been successful through good years and lean ones. He did well even when other merchants had economic difficulties. A friend once asked why he was successful when those about him failed. He replied that it was because of his attitude during those periods of apparent failure.

At the end of a season when he had a stock of goods left over, he charged off his loss at once. He did not carry over the old evaluation on a new inventory. Because of this his books always showed what his sound assets were. He was able to conduct his business successfully on the basis of the true value of his assets as he released the apparent business failures or mistakes of the past. *This businessman refused to brood over past mistakes. He loosed them, released them, and let them go. Because of this attitude, he was successful through good and lean years, even when fellow merchants continued to have financial problems.*

How often we have clung to our apparent mistakes, clasped them to us, kept them with us, rather than daring to do as this businessman did: let them go, knowing they were only misunderstood experiences which could still bring good to us. As that businessman proved, *every year can be a good year when you let go of that which has proved of little value to you, rather than carrying it over into the next year.*

HOW HE CLEARED TURMOIL OUT OF HIS LIFE

It is significant that Joshua had this experience with the people of Gibeon, because the word "Gibeon" symbolizes "a place of sacrifice in which man lets go." In dealing success-fully with the Gibeonites, Joshua had to let go the idea of mistakes, and so must we.

If you face difficulties of any sort and feel that if you had done differently it would now be well with you, then remind yourself that Universal Intelligence never makes mistakes. If an ever-present Universal Intelligence within and around you never makes mistakes, then no mistakes have been made!

A good way to look at apparent mistakes is this: Nothing is evil that brings forth good. The way to handle apparent evil in one's life is to give it "the light touch."

When you are inclined to attack your problems with the fury of a winter storm, remind yourself that it is the light touch of the warm spring breeze that dissipates the snow and dissolves the ice. Dwell upon the thought of universal good. Declare that something good is coming from that experience. This will turn the situation around and bring healing.

There once was a businessman who had been giving his full attention to the problems in his life. Then he turned his attention around by saying, *"I am one with God's universal goodness. Therefore, order and well-being now reign in me and in my world."* He was able to relax, to think clearly, and to handle his affairs with the light touch. The turmoil and frustration faded away.

You can give apparent mistakes and failures of the past or present "the light touch" as you declare often these words: *"I am a part of all that's good, and good shall still be victorious in this experience (or situation) now."*

HOW TO RESTORE ORDER IN YOUR WORLD

In his essay entitled *Compensation,*[1] Emerson gave some advice on how to gain a true perspective about apparent mistakes:

> "Our strength grows out of our weakness . . . Every evil to which we do not succumb is a benefactor . . . If I lose any good, I gain some other . . . No man ever had a defect that was not somewhere made useful to him . . . Things refuse to be mismanaged for long . . . For every apparent failure, there is also an equal success. A perfect equity adjusts its balance in all parts of life . . . The world looks like a multiplication table, which, turn it how you will, balances itself."

To realize that there are no mistakes—only experiences that were misunderstood—restores all things to their divine order. The tendency of the universe is toward perfection. Everything is striving to perfect itself. God's universal good for you extends into every department of your life—even into apparent mistakes! To help you claim such universal goodness declare, *"My good was all-powerful in that experience. My good still appears from that experience."*

---

1. *The Writings of Ralph Waldo Emerson* (New York, N.Y.: Random House, 1940).

HOW SHE TURNED A MISTAKE INTO A PROSPEROUS MARRIAGE

A businesswoman proved that there is a restoring power in realizing that there are no mistakes; that this realization restores all things to divine order; that the tendency of the universe is always toward perfection; and that a universal good can be all-powerful in all kinds of experiences.

This lady vacationed in a part of the United States where she had not previously visited. While there she became ill and obtained treatment which improved her condition, but did not heal it. She might have labeled her illness the result of mistaken, negative thinking. She might have brooded, "Why did this happen to me? What was wrong in my thinking that brought on this illness? What mistakes have I made mentally for which I am now paying?" She might have considered the whole experience a mistake, and she might have condemned herself for it, which would have been the greatest mistake of all.

But instead of calling her ill health the result of mistaken thinking she attended some church services in an effort to uplift her thinking. She kept saying privately, "That was not a negative experience because something good can still come from it."

At those church services, she met a doctor and felt guided to mention her health problem to him. He advised, "Come and see me. I believe I can help you." When she did, his treatments successfully cleared up her health problem. Having many mutual interests, they became friends. Later they married. What started out to be a negative experience turned into a great blessing when she refused to label it a "mistake."

HOW SHE RECEIVED A WEDDING GIFT TWENTY YEARS LATER

If there is some experience in your life which you have labeled a "mistake," then change the label! Remind yourself that a "mistake" is only an experience that has been misunderstood. *Something good can come from that experience once you take the negative label off of it.*

A lawyer's wife learned this idea and decided to relabel an experience she had had twenty years previously. She had worked for a struggling young attorney. When she married he had been financially unable to give her a wedding gift. Over a twenty-year period she had continued to think of him as a failure.

She decided to relabel her thoughts about him, naming him a "success." When she did so an amazing thing happened: A note soon arrived from him explaining that at the time of her marriage, he had not been able to give her a wedding gift, and this still bothered him. He wrote that he was now sending along that belated gift in appreciation for her faithful years of service in his office prior to her marriage. When the wedding gift arrived — twenty years later — it was a beautiful piece of silver.

HOW AN ACCIDENT RESULTED IN A HAPPY MARRIAGE

A businessman was involved in an automobile accident in which his health, and that of the driver of the other car, were both impaired. There were months of hospitalization and recuperation at home before this man was able to return to work.

His first impulse was to label this experience a negative one, but he realized that something good could still come from it. His hospitalization and recuperation periods were well covered financially by insurance. During this quiet period he rested, relaxed, read and reflected upon a number of subjects which interested him. He had time to enjoy the little pleasures of daily living, and to renew "the inner man."

As he continued to label this experience "good," he became better acquainted with the driver of the other car who had been involved in the same accident: She was a widowed businesswoman whom he might have negatively labeled as "a woman driver." She was also resting and recuperating from the experience. By the time they were both able to return to work, they had become engaged! They soon happily married. Again, what had seemed a negative experience produced a blessing for both of them. They proved that even *in the midst of apparent mistakes, things can still right themselves.*

HOW TO COPE SUCCESSFULLY WITH ADVERSITY

A famous educator was once asked how she accounted for her success in helping "bad boys." She replied, "I am successful because they are not 'bad boys.'" She refused to label them as such.

As long as you hold onto mistakes, magnify them, and feed them with the attention of your thoughts, they will be with you and may even continue to multiply in your life.

But the moment you rise up in your thinking to pronounce such mistakes "good," they begin to recede and disappear from your life. Only the blessing remains.

Stop feeling your difficulties deeply. Stop dramatizing them. Stop talking about them. Turn away from them, release them, and take hold of your thinking. Through use of these statements, you can successfully cope with adversity:

"As a beloved child of God, I am not meant to be a servant to trouble, adversity or sorrow. I am meant to be master of all the good that life has to offer! Mastery, dominion and authority are my divine heritage. So I now claim the peace, joy and abundance that are mine by divine right."

Strife added to strife only produces super-strife. How much better it is to say, *"I cannot recapture the past, but I have this hour and all the hours ahead. Through them divine restoration is now taking place. Yes, my good is being divinely restored to me now."*

Problems come to teach us something we need to know. If we are aware of this, the experience itself need not trouble us. Its negative aspects need scarcely make an impression, as we get busy drawing forth the good from it with this thought: *"This experience has come to teach me something good I need to know, so I accept the good from it and all else fades away."*

HANGING ONTO MISTAKES CAN BE A NEUROTIC CRUTCH

Where apparent mistakes are concerned, remember this: There are problems that result — not from a wrong attitude toward life — but from the necessity for growth. As our good unfolds, it sometimes presents problems to us that seem as difficult as any that life can offer, but they are actually blessings not understood so we ignorantly label them "mistakes."

Plato spoke of two kinds of blindness that affect mankind: (1) the blindness of going from light into darkness; (2) the blindness of coming from darkness into the light. The problems that occur when our good is being born is that of coming from darkness into the light — the light that our soul-growth demands.

Paul pointed this out when he said, "To them that love God all things work together for good." (Romans 8:28)

Some people get neurotic pleasure out of blaming themselves, condemning themselves, censoring themselves, or saying they have made mistakes. Such people tend to use mistakes as an emotional crutch. They feed emotionally on those negative experiences. They use those "mistakes" as an excuse for failure.

No matter how justified you may feel in doing so, you will never have a healthy normal life in the present if you hold onto unhealthy emotional memories from the past.

HOW TO PROSPER FROM MISTAKES

Like Joshua at Gibeon, when you stop condemning yourself, you are then able to draw forth the good from apparent mistakes. You can do it as you remind yourself that out of weakness comes strength; out of apparent failure arises success; that no matter what has happened in your life, God's unlimited good has the power to still appear and balance those experiences; that the tendency of the whole

universe is toward perfection; that mistakes are simply misunderstood experiences in one's soul-growth; that every apparent evil to which you do not succumb becomes a bene-
factor!

You can begin proving that there are no mistakes in life
as you dwell often upon these statements:

*"Nothing is evil that brings forth good. I rename this
experience a 'success.' I draw forth the good from all apparent mistakes of past or present. Something good still comes
from each experience. God's goodness is all-powerful so I
pronounce each experience good. Then I leave it alone.
The goodness of God now extends into every department of
my life. For every apparent failure, there is an equal success. God makes no mistakes and produces no failures. I am
a complete success because God made me!"*

SUMMARY

1. Many a mistake has been built upon an apparent failure. The word "mistake" means "misunderstood." Your mistakes are merely experiences which you have misunderstood.

2. The next town to be captured was the royal city of Gibeon, a stronghold in the Promised Land. The people of Gibeon were frightened by the powerful Hebrews, so they decided to outwit Joshua rather than fight his army.

3. As though they were from a far country, the Gibeonites dressed themselves in muddy old clothes. This ragged, hungry group then appeared in Joshua's camp and asked to make a treaty, in which they would become allies with the Hebrews.

4. In the treaty, Joshua agreed that the Gibeonites would never be killed by the Hebrews. He soon discovered the ragged strangers were only from Gibeon, the next town to be conquered.

5. Since Joshua had made a sacred pledge not to kill their people, he kept it even though they had tricked him.

6. Something good came from this apparent mistake. The Hebrews then took the town of Gibeon without losing a single life. The Gibeonites became servants of the Hebrews.

7. Gibeon was a prosperous town worth saving because it opened the rich trade routes throughout the Promised Land. Joshua's apparent mistake proved not to be a bad bargain. Because of the thriving trade routes that

were opened throughout the Promised Land, unprecedented prosperity was established for the Hebrews.

8. From Joshua we learn there are no mistakes; only experiences which we have not understood, so we give them a false interpretation. We label them evil when there is good in them.

9. Refuse to brood over past mistakes. Loose them, release them, let them go. Every year can be a good year when you let go of that which has proved of little value to you, rather than carrying it over into the next year.

10. Problems come to teach us something we need to know. To realize there are no mistakes, only experiences that were misunderstood, restores all things to their divine order. Something good can come from that experience once you take the negative label off of it.

HOW TO GAIN CONTROL AND PROSPER

— Chapter 8 —

As he swept through the Promised Land, Joshua's conquests included these:

First: He took Jericho with no implements of war.

Second: His men tried to take the town of Ai and were defeated — until they found and punished the thief in their midst. Then they were successful.

Third: The people of Gibeon, the royal city in the heart of the Promised Land, tricked Joshua into making a treaty with them so that he would not destroy them. As a result, Joshua took Gibeon — without war — through a peaceful invasion. This opened up rich trade routes throughout the Promised Land so that its conquest proved to be a vast prosperity blessing.

There were five kings in the Promised Land who heard of Joshua's victories. They decided that the only way to overcome Joshua was by forming an alliance to work together to defeat him. These five kings were determined to put Joshua's army to flight. (Joshua 10)

But Joshua surprised the five kings. He made an all-night march and attacked them at dawn when their armies were still sleeping. There was little fighting because Joshua caught them unprepared, and their surprised troops ran away.

They fled into the hill country and into the mountain passes near Gibeon at a place called Bethhoron. Then complex fighting resulted because Joshua's men had to go after the enemy in the hills and mountains. It wasn't as simple as meeting them as one united army in the valley.

While the troops of the five kings went in all directions and fought Joshua's army in the hills and mountains around Bethhoron, the five kings escaped and hid themselves in a cave. But Joshua's men discovered where they were, sealed off the cave with huge stones, and then continued fighting the armies of the five kings.

THE UNIVERSAL IMPORTANCE OF THE BATTLE OF BETHHORON

The Battle of Bethhoron has been called "one of the world's great battles." Certainly it was one of the most famous in history. The Battle of Bethhoron was one of the few military engagements that belonged equally to ecclesiastical and to civil history. It was one of the few in which the fortunes of the world and that of the church were equally decided.

It was *the* decisive battle for the Hebrews, because it was their last great fight toward freedom and independence.

The whole future of the Hebrews as a race and as a religion rested upon whether they won this battle. All that they had accomplished since leaving Egypt and entering into the Promised Land could be undone if they were defeated now.

Joshua knew that if he could break the strength of the five kings in battle, their strength would be broken forever. Complete possession of the Promised Land would be assured.

There had to be victory at Bethhoron or all would be forever lost for the Hebrews in the Promised Land. It was a matter of "demonstrating or else" — of finishing the fight "or else." History reveals that such crucial wars have often been a factor in the development of civilization — another instance in which we see that out of what appears to be evil can still come forth something good.

PROSPERITY FROM THE BATTLE OF BETHHORON

When we have reached a decisive point in our lives and have to get results "or else" — we should follow Joshua's example.

Things began to look crucial in this battle because the end of the day was coming, and there were still many of the enemy troops in the hills and mountain passes that had not been captured.

Joshua knew that if darkness came before the enemy was captured, they might escape. So he called upon the sun and moon to stand still; he asked that the day be prolonged so that a complete victory might be obtained.

Joshua did nothing complicated in order to produce what seemed miraculous at this point. He used the same power

184 THE MILLIONAIRE JOSHUA

that you and I use every day. Joshua declared: "Sun, stand
thou still upon Gibeon. And thou, moon, in the valley of
Aijalon." (Joshua 10;12)

The results?

"The sun stood still, and the moon stayed, until the
nation had avenged itself of its enemies." (Joshua 10:13)

Here is another example of the power of one's words to
control the events of one's life: As a result of those simple
decrees, it remained bright daylight for another twelve
hours. Joshua's men were able to continue their attacks, and
they were victorious. When the sun finally went down, the
Hebrews were masters of the entire Promised Land. It was a
prosperity conquest that has never been equalled!

Their desire of many centuries had finally come about.
But at the decisive moment, their dreams had come true
only after they remembered to take control of their destiny
by speaking forth definite words. The almighty "power of
the word" had triumphed again!

HOW YOU CAN USE THEIR SUCCESS SECRET

When you are trying to make a "master demonstration,"
it may seem that you have that one last hurdle to overcome. That is your decisive period. That is your battle of
Bethhoron. Don't give up. Don't turn back. Instead, speak
the word of complete victory and fulfillment: *This is a
time of divine fulfillment. This is a time of complete victory now.*

Or declare that you have time for everything. A businesswoman in Michigan wrote:

"My daily statements that *'everything is working out for good under divine timing.'* have been very effective. A court case has righted itself. The latest physical exam revealed that my health has vastly improved; that *'every day in every way, I am getting better and better.'* Thanks to the 'divine timing' statements, I am calmer, and new things are happening for good in my life."

THE DEEPER MEANING OF THIS BATTLE

Sometimes we are tested that one last time. The place where this last decisive battle took place—"Bethhoron"— has special meaning that explains why you may have to decree good for yourself that one last time in order to achieve victory.

The word "Bethhoron" means "a thought center deep in consciousness, in which the higher thoughts of justice and truth may descend in order to cleanse erroneous thoughts and emotions."

When you speak positive words that one last time and decree that your good is coming forth, it is then that your words go to that thought center deep within you. The higher thoughts of justice and truth descend into the inner levels of your mind and emotions, clearing out limited beliefs as well as negative emotions, and preparing for victorious results.

Just as Joshua's men needed more time and more daylight to search out the enemy from the hill country and mountain passes, sometimes your deliberate good words need one last chance to go deep within your thinking, to search out and cleanse the mind of fragments of negative thought lodged there from the past.

Just one more session of speaking good words may bring the decisive victory you need, or the long-awaited good you've worked for.

So never underestimate the power of constructive, faith-filled words. There is an almost fantastic power of achievement released through the deliberate speaking forth of good words. Joshua knew about the atomic power of words and used them to produce a mighty result. You can, too!

HOW THE ATOMIC POWER OF WORDS PROSPERED, GUIDED, AND HEALED THEM

SHE GOT WORK IN TEXAS: "I had prayed the usual ways and nothing happened. Then I began to declare every day: *'Divine love is now working perfectly through me toward all people. Divine love is now working perfectly through all people toward me.'* Things started to happen right away: I received a much-needed teaching position; the flow of private students through my music studio at home commenced once more. *Although I had read endless self-help books, nothing helped me until I began to speak forth definite words.*"

FOOD CAME TO SENIOR CITIZENS IN CALIFORNIA: "I had prayed for a greater income for us, but there were no results until I began to declare daily, *'I do not depend upon persons or conditions for our prosperity. God is the source of our supply, and God provides his own amazing channels of supply to us now. From every point of the universe, our good comes to us in abundance!'*

"Our Senior Citizens group was soon invited to participate in the receipt of fresh vegetables and fruits donated by the many growers in the Salinas and San Joaquin Valleys nearby. We get enough each week to supply our needs for many days. There is ample to share with neighbors who are not in the program. In turn, my neighbors who know I do not drive, often stop by to offer me a ride or to shop for me. Since I began declaring, *'Our good comes to us now!'* my husband has begun to recover from a severe stroke. *Only God knows how much good has come to us since I began to declare it."*

SHE WAS SUPPLIED AMID SHORTAGES IN NEW YORK: "During a period of shortages, I found everything I needed by declaring daily, *'I turn the great energy of my thinking upon ideas of plenty, and I now have plenty—regardless of what people about me are doing or saying. I am abundantly supplied now!'"*

THE BILLS GOT PAID IN WASHINGTON: "The nicest things have happened to me financially since I began to hold our bills in my hands and declare daily, *'I give thanks for the immediate, complete payment of all financial obligations now, quickly and in peace.'* An old insurance policy even paid off! This is most amazing since it was a company that had gone out of business and I had been assured no repayment was possible."

A HOUSEWIFE GOT WORK IN CONNECTICUT: "I spoke the word for *'the perfect job with the perfect pay.'* I needed work during the day while my children were in school. Within twenty-four hours after declaring those words, I found a job at the neighborhood restaurant as a short-order cook and waitress from 10-3:00 daily. This convenient job takes the strain off our family's financial affairs and will provide us with many extras. *It is good to know we have a loving Father who will take care of us when we decree it."*

NEW BEAUTY IN NEW YORK: The statement *'I give thanks for ever-increasing health, youth and beauty'* led me to a beauty shop I had not visited in ten years. A brand-new hair style, which has made all the difference in my looks and personality, has been the happy result. I feel younger and more prosperous, too."

HE RECEIVED NEW CAR, HOME AND TRAVEL IN CANADA: "Since I began to declare every day, *'I am beautifully and appropriately supplied with the rich substance of the universe now,'* how I have prospered! More pay, a new car, a new home, and extended travel have all come to me."

HIS JOB WAS RESTORED IN SRI LANKA: "I used the statement, *'I am now guided into my true place with the true people and with the true prosperity.'* The result was that I have been re-employed by my old company. It is an excellent job that I held up until five years ago. Although certain of my business associates have gone ahead of me in seniority, I am delighted to be back with the firm. It is the best job I have ever had with excellent fringe benefits."

HE RECEIVED $75 IN AFRICA: "I received a gift of $75 soon after I began to declare *'I rejoice because my prayers are now answered. My dreams are now coming true!'* This is all the more amazing since I am a member of a 'non-profit' profession (a minister) in this poverty-stricken part of the world."

THE HEALING OF A PAINFUL INJURY IN TEXAS: "Four years ago I was injured when I fell on the ice. Although I had had periods of improvement, I had not been healed. Recently I began to declare, *'Nobody and nothing is bigger than God, and He is healing me now.'* The pain left my hip and has not returned. Praise God."

HOW TO AVOID THE HIGH PRICE OF NO RESULTS

There are those skeptics who doubt that Joshua had the power to make time stand still. They try to explain it away in some manner. Yet historians assure us that it actually happened; that a miracle *did* take place.

History reveals that *when God was on the side of the Hebrews, they won—even in the face of insurmountable challenges. The universe shared in their battles and rejoiced in their victories!* Joshua proved that popular metaphysical saying, "There is no time in Spirit." What does this mean?

In the very beginning you were created in the image and likeness of God and given dominion over everything in the universe, including time. This means that there is no time on the spiritual plane so you have time for everything— everything important. But you must claim it.

If you do not seem to have time for everything, then like Joshua, you can take control of the elements by telling the sun and moon to stand still. How? By decreeing, *"I have time for everything that is important and necessary to the divine plan of my life. This is a time of divine completion now."*

People who know about the power that they can release through their thoughts and words should be discriminating. They should not waste their time on unnecessary activities or unimportant events in life.

When you are not getting the results you feel you should have, this may be the reason: You may be wasting your time

and substance on people, situations, or experiences that are
unimportant and unnecessary in your life.

You may have allowed other people to drain you emotionally, physically or financially, and then wondered why you
had not gotten the results you should have had. You may
have wasted your time and substance in "riotous living" and
paid "the high price of no results" for that wasted time and
effort.

However, since the universe shares in your battles and
rejoices in your victories, there is a solution.

HOW TO HAVE TIME FOR EVERYTHING

You will have time for everything that is necessary and
important to your life when you do the important things,
and let everything and everybody else go. Dare to say "No"
to people who try to take your time, energy or funds unnec-
essarily. They will not long be offended by your lack of
attention because they will go elsewhere for it.

You waste time when you become a *physical* slave to
others and you pay a high price for such foolishness. Respect
yourself. Serve and help, but never be a slave. You cannot
help others by doing for them those things which they
should be doing for themselves. You inflict injury upon a
person when you wait on him too much. You can serve
others by showing them how to help themselves, but not by
doing it for them.

You waste time when you become a slave to others *emo-*
tionally, and you pay a high price for such waste. Do not
make the mistake of being enslaved to the opinions of
others, or of enslaving them to yours. Do not become uneasy

over the failures and mistakes of others. Do not feel you must interfere. Do not be disturbed if others seem to go wrong. Do not feel that you must step in and set them right.

Each person is unfolding according to the level of his understanding — not according to your understanding — and you must let him. Do not meddle in the personal habits of others, though those involved are dear to you.

You can shine the light *on* a person but not in him or for him. Release everyone around you to their own growth in their own way. Bless them, behold the good in them, picture progress for them, pray for them, but refrain from criticism and interference. Do the things that are right for you to do, and declare that all others are following the pathways that are best for them. Declare often, *"I am in true relationship with all people and all situations now. All people and all situations are in true relationship with me now."*

I have often seen things right themselves quickly for others when I have declared, *"All things conform to the right thing for you now quickly and in peace,"* and then released those involved to their perfect outworking.

Be careful that you do not enslave others by your notions of what is right or wrong for them. Try to help all who come to you in inner ways, but do not go about officiously trying to set other people right in outer ways. It is not your mission in life to physically correct people's morals, habits or life styles. Mind your own business. As you personally lead a constructive life, you need not preach to others. You will help them far more than the person who preaches continually, but who leads a petty, interfering life.

HOW TO AVOID HURRY AND PROSPER

Do not be a slave to time either. Hurry is a manifestation of fear. He who fears not has plenty of time. Declare that you are never too late or too early, and that nothing will go wrong. When you find yourself getting excited, worried or in a mental attitude of hurry declare, *"Peace, order and harmony are now established and maintained."* Refuse to hurry; sit down, relax, exercise, meditate, read, play a game or even go on a trip—but do not be a slave to time.

There are prosperous reasons why you should avoid hurry: *The negative vibrations of hurry instantly cut your connection with universal good.* You will have to work twice as hard for half as much if you hurry. You will not have the power or wisdom needed to prosper unless you remain calm, relaxed, harmonious and unhurried.

The hurried, agitated state of mind is powerless to produce good in your life. Fear and hurry turn strength into weakness. They repel your good rather than attract it. But the calm, peaceful, unhurried state of mind is all powerful to gather the wealth of the universe and produce prosperous results for you.

"We travel farthest when we make haste slowly," is a Roman proverb that has helped me. Since I have simplified my schedule and worked in a quieter, more unhurried way, I have accomplished far more with far less strain. Prosperity has come for all concerned in easier, more satisfying ways.

It is appropriate that we should learn this particular success secret toward the end of Joshua's long career, after

he had led the Hebrews in claiming their long-desired Land
of Canaan. As mentioned often throughout this book, the
word "Canaan" significantly means "the realm of substance
which is the foundation of all wealth."

Yes, hurry dissipates that rich universal substance.
Whereas, the peaceful, unhurried state of mind attracts its
vast benefits. The Hebrews were destined to prove this, and
so can you!

In the popular, much quoted poem entitled, "I Didn't
Have Time," its unknown author describes how we can
begin to claim vast benefits in our lives:

> I got up early one morning
>   and rushed right into the day!
> I had so much to accomplish
>   that I didn't have time to pray.
> Problems just tumbled about me
>   and heavier came each task.
> 'Why doesn't God help me?' I wondered.
> He answered 'You didn't ask.'
> I tried to come into God's presence.
> I used all my keys at the lock.
> God gently and lovingly chided,
>   'Why, child, you didn't knock.'
> I wanted to see joy and beauty.
> But the day toiled on, grey and bleak.
> I wondered why God didn't show me.
> He said, 'But you didn't seek!'
> I woke up early this morning;
>   and paused before entering the day.
> I had so much to accomplish
>   that I *had* to take time to pray!

What a difference it makes when we choose to do some
quiet mental work first before facing the day. *Those quiet*

times of prayer, inspirational study, speaking forth positive words of good, and meditating become the most precious periods of our day, and the most productive of good. When you make a practice of it, you can understand why some authorities claim that what usually takes a person six hours to do could easily be accomplished in one hour by a person who knew how to pray and meditate first! It is a soul-satisfying, age-old method that can help us to avoid hurry and worry, and to prosper.

THE BENEFITS OF PSYCHOLOGICAL WARFARE

Not only did time stand still for the Hebrews, but the battle of Bethhoron was a miracle in other ways, too. Joshua used psychological warfare to achieve this victory. The Hebrews were greatly outnumbered from the start. The enemy consisted of the five kings and their large armies. Not only did Joshua's men triumph over the enemy, but they returned to the cave in which the five kings were sealed and destroyed them, too. "And all these kings and their land did Joshua take at one time, because Jehovah, the God of Israel, fought for Israel." (Joshua 10:42)

There were still some thirty-odd rulers in the Promised Land. When they heard what had happened to the five kings, they surrendered on Joshua's terms. By destroying the five kings, Joshua avoided further battle and bloodshed with the other rulers in the Promised Land. There were local skirmishes, but no more major battles. Historians feel that he saved many lives by sacrificing those of the five leaders. His decision wrought innumerable benefits of peace and plenty to the whole Promised Land. Afterwards, Joshua was victorious in the conquest of all the hill country, too. "So Joshua took the whole land . . . Joshua gave it for an inheritance unto Israel . . . And the land had rest from war." (Joshua 11:23)

At this point, *all* of the abundance that Joshua viewed in the Promised Land was but a small part of the greater prosperity mission which his life's work had set in motion for the Hebrews. Joshua had achieved the prosperity that Moses had promised the Hebrews so many years before:

> *"Jehovah thy God bringeth thee into a good land,* a land of brooks of water, of fountains and springs, flowing forth in valleys and hills; a land of wheat and barley, vines, fig trees, and pomegranates; a land of olive trees and honey; *a land wherein thou shalt eat bread without scarceness, thou shalt not lack anything in it;* a land whose stones are iron, and out of whose hills thou mayest dig copper. *And thou shalt eat and be full and thou shalt bless Jehovah thy God for the good land which he hath given thee."*
> (Deuteronomy 8:7-10)

As you meditate upon the foregoing description of the abundance that Moses had earlier prophesied for the Hebrews—and which they now enjoyed—I trust you will realize that it is a symbolic description of all the abundance that has been prophesied for you, too!

As you use Joshua's prosperity secrets which have been described in this book, your own true abundance will be revealed to you. Indeed my prayer for you is this: *"May Jehovah thy God bring thee into a good land. A land wherein thou shalt eat bread without scarceness. Thou shalt not lack anything in it."*

SUMMARY

1. Five kings formed an alliance in an effort to defeat Joshua's army. But through a surprise attack by his army at dawn, their troops fled into the hill country at Bethhoron.

2. The Battle of Bethhoron was *the* decisive battle for the Hebrews, because it was their last great fight toward freedom and independence.

3. Joshua knew that if he could break the strength of these five kings in battle, complete possession of the Promised Land was assured.

4. There were still many enemy troops to be captured toward the end of the day. So Joshua called upon the sun and moon to stand still. He asked that the day be prolonged so that a complete victory might be obtained.

5. As a result of his simple decrees, bright daylight remained for another twelve hours. Joshua's men were victorious. When the sun set, the Hebrews were masters of the entire Promised Land. It was a prosperity conquest that has never been equalled.

6. The word "Bethhoron" means "a thought center deep in consciousness, in which the higher thoughts of justice and truth may descend in order to cleanse erroneous thoughts and emotions."

7. Just as Joshua's men needed more time to search out the enemy, sometimes your deliberate good words need one last chance to go deep within your thinking and cleanse it of fragments of negative thought, to clear the way for results.

8. One more session of speaking good words may bring the decisive victory you need. So never underestimate the power of constructive, faith-filled words.

9. When you are not getting the results you feel you should have, it may be that you are wasting your time and substance on people, situations or experiences that are unimportant and unnecessary in your life.

10. The negative vibrations of hurry instantly cut your connections with universal good. Whereas, the peaceful, unhurried state of mind attracts its vast benefits.

11. Those quiet times of prayer, inspirational study, speaking positive words of good, and meditation become the most precious periods in our day, and the most productive of good.

12. A psychological victory was achieved at Bethhoron. When the thirty-odd rulers heard of the Hebrews' victory at Bethhoron, they surrendered. Many lives were saved. The innumerable benefits of peace and plenty came to the Promised Land.

THE PROSPERITY LAW OF CHANGE

— Chapter 9 —

A successful businesswoman recently stated that she insists upon making a change in her life every six or seven years. If change does not begin to work through the normal course of events, she deliberately invokes a change. She stated that this action has always brought satisfying results. "I refuse to settle down in a rut. I refuse to stagnate," she commented.

At the age of 82, a distinguished photographer, painter and art critic gave this sage advice:

"When you begin to feel stale, give yourself a swift kick in the pants before somebody else does it for you! We all need change. It shakes us up, gives us a new look at things, and keeps us alive. It can be change of inlook or outlook, a change of reading habits, a change of social activities, a change of diet, a change of residence, or a change of jobs.

Change is growth. Change is living. I am 82 years old and still changing."

As a tribute to this man's remarkable success, an exhibition of his photography was held at the New York Museum of Modern Art—on his 82nd birthday!

JOSHUA ON THE SUCCESS POWER OF CHANGE

In the Bible, the passing away of one leader and the rise of another symbolized the changes through which the progressive person passes on the eternal journey into his ever-expanding good.

The great warrior, Joshua, teaches us much about the success power of change. After he took the Hebrews into their Promised Land, Joshua then spent the next seven years helping them take possession of it; more than thirty kings and chieftains were defeated in the process. By the time this mission was completed, Joshua was between 90 and 100 years of age.

In the accomplishment of his prosperity mission:

"Joshua left nothing undone of all that the Lord commanded Moses . . . Joshua took the whole land according to all that the Lord said unto Moses; and Joshua gave it for an inheritance to Israel . . ."
(Joshua 11:15,23)

What a lavish gift this represented—one of billionaire proportions—and how casually he shared it! After this prosperity mission was accomplished, Joshua spent his last years quietly establishing peace and order. Once the Land of

Canaan had been possessed, he divided the property and gave each of the Hebrew tribes their rightful portion.

The first assignment of land went, appropriately, to the staunch and loyal Caleb, who had so faithfully helped Joshua to carry out his high mission. Caleb had been one of the original twelve spies whom Moses had sent out of the wilderness to spy on the Promised Land. It had been the positive thinking Caleb who had returned to enthusiastically declare, "Let us go up at once and possess it; for we are well able to overcome it." (Numbers 13:30) "The land, which we passed through to spy it out, is an exceeding good land. If Jehovah delight in us, then he will bring us into this land and give it to us; a land which floweth with milk and honey," (Numbers 14:7-9) Whereas the ten negative-thinking spies died in the wilderness, Caleb was destined to accompany Joshua into the Promised Land in triumph.

In appreciation for his lifelong loyalty and help, Joshua graciously bestowed upon the prosperous-thinking Caleb the rich vineyard hill country of Hebron, which was considered one of the most important areas in the territory of Judah. The bountiful springs of water found there, which the generous Caleb quickly shared with his relatives, indicates the vast wealth of that area. (Joshua 15:19) Caleb enjoyed his well-earned prosperity in the Promised Land. At the age of 85, he was still strong and vigorous: "I am as strong this day as I was in the day that Moses sent me; as my strength was then, even so is my strength now." (Joshua 14:11)

It is significant that, under Joshua's leadership, a portion of the Promised Land was set aside for the female descendants. Not only the sons, but the daughters, were to share in the inheritance. This was a great step forward because the women had earlier been placed in the same category as the cattle. (Exodus 20:17) Now they were given the right to inherit! (Joshua 17:3,4)

After establishing "divine order" among his followers in their new surroundings, Joshua then retired to the hill country of northern Palestine, where he serenely viewed the rich Promised Land that he had proudly won for his people.

When Joshua felt the change of death near, he did as Moses had done before him: he called the people together, and reminded them of all they had accomplished with God's help. He admonished them to keep close to God if they wished to maintain their victories:

> "Fear (revere) Jehovah and serve Him in sincerity and in truth . . . Choose you this day whom ye will serve . . . As for me and my house, we will serve Jehovah."
>
> (Joshua 24:14,15)

His farewell address expressed the same noble, courageous spirit that had animated his entire life. In his farewell address he reminded the Hebrews that it had not been Israel's sword that had been the secret for their success in taking the Promised Land; their true success had a spiritual basis; God had been the source of their supply and enduring success. This same basic success secret was to lead them to phenomenal success in the years to come!

Joshua did not resist nor resent the change that was coming for him and his followers. He knew that change was a time of growth; that change was good and necessary, both for him and for the Hebrews. His followers did not resent it either. Instead, they welcomed change and responded positively to it.

After Joshua's death, the Hebrews were ready to progress more on an individual basis. Instead of appointing another strong leader, they appointed judges to rule each of their twelve tribes.

HOW CHANGE IS A SUCCESS POWER

We can learn an important success secret from the Hebrews' non-resistant attitudes toward change:

In order to grow we, too, have to meet change many times in life. *The human nature of man is inclined to resist change, though the spiritual nature of man insists upon it. To resist change is to stop your growth. A change indicates that "your growing is showing." So you should welcome change and call it good!* It was the illustrious writer, Emmet Fox, who once said, "I see the angel of God in every change."

The soul demands change for its expansion. In the midst of change, the creation of new good takes place. The death of the old is but the birth of the new.

You should never become bound to former ideas, relationships, or environments. As you expand your thinking, some old relationships and ways of living will probably drop away from you, but only to be replaced by new, more understanding ones.

You should not allow yourself to become so fixed to certain ways of living that you cannot be happy when those ways change, as they surely will.

Remind yourself often that all things work together for good, even amid changes. *If the caterpillar could refuse to change, it would miss becoming a butterfly!* The person who tries to avoid change often stagnates into experiences of loss, lack, and failure. *Change cannot be by-passed. It can only be temporarily avoided.*

A mystical statement that has meant much to me over the years is this: "When the soul is ready for the next step in its upward growth, a great change takes place." *The soul of man goes through many changes in the course of a lifetime, if that person is growing, expanding and making progress.* Emerson wrote:[1]

"In proportion to the vigor of the individual these revolutions are frequent . . . The changes which break up at short intervals the prosperity of men are advertisements of a nature whose law is growth."

Change is the master law of life since it is the law of nature to grow. To live is to grow and to grow is to change.

Emerson advised that we should be putting off "dead circumstances" daily, but that we have often resisted doing so. Then our growth came in shocks. He wrote:[2]

"We are idolators of the old . . . We do not believe there is any force in today to rival or re-create that beautiful yesterday. We linger in the ruins . . . We sit and weep in vain. The voice of the Almighty saith, 'Up and onward forever more!' We cannot stay amid the ruins."

How do these changes come? Perhaps through ill health, disappointment, loss of wealth, family or friends. Often the loss seems unbearable. Yet such losses work "revolutions" in

1. Ralph Waldo Emerson, *The Writings of Ralph Waldo Emerson* (New York, N.Y.: Random House, 1940).
2. Ibid.

our way of life. They force the termination of an era that was waiting to be closed: a wornout occupation, household or life style ends. This allows the formation of new ones "more friendly to the character."[3]

Furthermore, such drastic changes open the way for the formation of a new way of life that "proves of the first importance to the next years."[4]

Perhaps you have discovered that letting go of the old is usually harder than taking hold of the new. When you are in the midst of change and are finding it difficult to let go, read Emerson's complete description of the necessity and blessing of change as given in the latter part of his essay entitled *Compensation.*[5]

HOLD FAST AND FAIL, LET GO AND SUCCEED

These words of advice once caught my attention: "Hold fast and you fail. Let go and you grow into a greater success." To climb, one hand must go above the other. So it is in life. You succeed not by hanging fearfully to the old, but by reaching out mentally and taking new handholds. Dare to accept, welcome, and adapt new and better ideas. Hold fast and you fail. Let go and you grow into a greater success.

When you hold fast to the old, not only do you fail but you have to eventually let go anyway. If you resist change, your growth still comes but through unpleasant experiences. You will literally be shocked into letting go. We all agree

---

3. Ibid.
4. Ibid.
5. Ibid.

that change isn't always easy. As that 82-year old photographer stated, "It shakes us up."

Changes occur that sometimes seem bitter experiences, and it takes a strong belief in God's goodness to declare that only good shall come from such changes. Yet it always does come when there is a steadfast insistence that good is coming forth anyway. In his evolutionary growth and progress, man has always moved through cycles that led to change.

HOW TO RECOGNIZE CHANGE AT WORK

You may be thinking, "But how do I recognize change at work in my life? How do I know when it's coming?"

The first signs of change are the restlessness and dissatisfaction one begins to feel. When you get near the end of a cycle in your growth and progress, you become restless and dissatisfied with a situation that had previously been satisfactory.

Sooner or later, most of us come to a place in our development where we are no longer satisfied to go on living as we have in the past. When we first reach this point in our soul growth, we do not always know just what is taking place. In our restlessness, we may be tempted to think that our good has left us. Yet we will find that we are merely going from one room into a larger, better room of life.

There is another way you can recognize change: Not only do you become restless and dissatisfied with the old situation, but you often begin to fail in it. Nothing goes right any more. *You begin to fail where you had previously succeeded. That formerly successful situation becomes hostile, unfriendly, inharmonious to you. It no longer cooperates*

with you, because it is releasing you to your new good else-
where! When this happens, failure is success trying to be
born in a bigger way in your life, so let it!

Perhaps you had a job you liked, one in which you were
successful. After a fruitful, productive period you began to
fail in it. No more raises or financial recognition came to
you. Your co-workers no longer cooperated with you. They
may have even become critical of you as well as difficult to
work with. You wondered where you had failed, because
previously you had succeeded.

You have not failed! Those are the "dead circumstances"
which Emerson said must be cast off. *That situation has*
unconsciously released you to your greater good elsewhere.
If things had remained harmonious and cooperative, you
would not have made the effort to go through the change
that was necessary for your further growth and progress.

You had to be forced out of the old situation through
inharmonious, disappointing experiences of apparent failure—so the supposed failure was good. It forced you to do
what you should have done anyway. It forced you to do
what your soul was demanding: that a change take place.
At this point, if you had held fast you would have failed.
This was the time to "let go and grow."

HE WAS FORCED INTO A CHANGE THAT
BROUGHT SUCCESS

A businessman had long desired to become a success in
the oil business. But after repeated failure, he settled for a
college teaching job. He was trained for this work, but felt

limited in it both financially and in the use of his talents. He longed to return to the oil fields.

His college teaching job finally became so dissatisfying and so inharmonious that he was forced to resign. A business colleague suggested they go into the oil business together. Although this man had little money, his colleague provided the capital, whereas he provided years of knowledge and experience. This time his efforts in the oil business were fruitful. He proved that there comes a time when you must cast off "dead circumstances"; that if you hold fast you fail, but if you let go you grow and prosper.

THINGS THAT DROP AWAY FROM YOU ARE A PART OF YOUR SUCCESS

Old ways must often die. Failure is only the death of those old ways so that the new hundredfold increase of blessings may follow. At such times if you become frightened and discouraged, you miss the new good that is on its way to you.

When such transition periods come, if one particular talent is no longer needed, it may be because you had become so satisfied with that one ability that you had ceased to expand and grow in other ways. You may have gotten into a comfortable rut. Although you were unaware of it, your soul had been reaching out toward greater possibilities.

If you will not voluntarily get out of that comfortable rut after you have learned what is necessary along certain lines, things drop away from you in order that there may be room for further growth in other phases of your life.

Have you ever watched a gardener prune branches from trees and shrubs? Did it not appear that he was ruining the plants? Yet he was only cutting out the old dead wood to make room for new growth.

Any experience that causes you to grow in understanding is a successful experience. Apparently failures are only transition periods from an old cycle into a new one—from the lesser to the greater.

The human part of us likes to "settle down" and become fixed, remaining in a shell. But the old shell must be cast off to make way for a larger understanding. Apparent failure is the breaking up of the old shell so that the richer experiences of life may come to pass.

The philosopher, Kahlil Gibran,[6] described it:

"Your pain is the breaking of the shell that encloses your understanding."

When it seems you have "lost your hold" on a situation, it is because you are supposed to lose your hold on it! You are supposed to let it go so that new good may appear. You cannot stop change. You can only delay it and cause it to come through shocks and negative experiences that are not necessary if you will let go graciously.

HOW TO MEET CHANGE NONRESISTANTLY AND PROSPER

How do you meet change nonresistantly?

Joshua met the great change that came toward the end of

6. Reprinted from *The Prophet*, by Kahlil Gibran, with permission of the publisher, Alfred A. Knopf, Inc. Copyright 1923 by Kahlil Gibran; renewal copyright 1951 by Administrators C.T.A. of Kahlil Gibran estate, and Mary G. Gibran.

his life by living quietly in the hill country of northern Palestine. In view of the active life Joshua had led for so many years, that quiet latter part of his life reflected a vast change. It is significant that he later passed away on Mount Ephraim because the word "Ephraim" means "doubly fruitful," "very productive."

Changes in your life will be doubly fruitful and very productive if you, too, meet them quietly. When the pace slows down, that is the time for you to rest, relax, and listen for the inner promptings of Universal Intelligence. Such evening periods of peaceful rest may seem periods of failure in some ways. But quiet evening periods always precede busy morning periods of new activity, so enjoy them while they last.

Such a quiet period is a time when you are being allowed to gather your forces together for the greater expansion. The unfoldment of some other talents and abilities may be longing to be pushed through you into expression. The new talents or powers may differ greatly in their character from the former ones. Hence the rest and the quiet transition.

You should avoid doubting that your good is at work during transition periods. You should avoid fear of letting go of the lesser in order that the greater good may appear. Remind yourself of the words of a famed musician, "You can't play with the same toys all of your life."

Especially you should avoid running away from your own indwelling guidance to seek outside advice. This would only confuse you. Don't talk about the change that is working. Listen to your intuition or "inner teacher" and dare to follow through on its promptings. This is the wisdom of the universe speaking to you.

"There must be an inworking before there can be an outworking," declared one sage. Do not be discouraged or disheartened, but regard such quiet periods as a time of inworking.

At this point wholly trust God's goodness. Declare often: *"I willingly do the will of God in this situation."* Or *"God works in me to will and to do whatsoever He wishes me to do. God cannot fail, so I cannot fail."* Or from the Lord's prayer, *"Thy kingdom come. Thy will be done,"* since God's will for you is always unlimited good.

Like the people of Joshua's era, when you meet changes nonresistantly, your life becomes fruitful, satisfying and productive of good. Your "cup runneth over."

To help bring this about, you will enjoy declaring often these words: *"I meet life nonresistantly and my own life becomes fruitful, satisfying and productive of good. My 'cup runneth over.'"*

HOW THE AUTHOR'S LIFE IMPROVED THROUGH CHANGE

From my own experiences, I can personally attest to the vast improvement that change can bring into one's life. I took up the study of prosperous thinking while working in the business world in my home state of North Carolina, at a time when I was widowed with a young son to rear alone.

At the height of my job in those surroundings, I felt guided to start all over again in a new profession as a non-denominational minister. This led me away from family and friends to a new life in the beautiful state of Alabama. There I worked hard, lived meagerly and learned my new profession. There I met the severe recession of 1958 by teaching a prosperity class which was so successful that it led to the writing of numerous articles and several prosperity books.

Five years later, through marriage, I moved to the state of Texas. Two years later I was suddenly widowed again. There I continued to live quietly for more than a decade, establishing two new churches from financial scratch as well as researching and writing a number of books. I began to travel extensively during this period in connection with my books, and completed the raising of my son.

In recent years I have made another move, this time to the "Golden State" of California, a land of sunshine, tropical beauty, and vast physical and metaphysical wealth. Only now—for the first time—as I live and work in this metaphysical area, are my personal dreams beginning to come true. I feel as though I have finally entered my Promised Land where I belong.

Like Joshua, I have witnessed the necessity of change for one's growth and progress. Only now am I beginning to become established in my Promised Land. Yet all that has happened over several decades has been a series of steps leading me to this point in my soul growth where true personal success is now possible.

How I appreciate the warrior, Joshua—and his daring spirit—which would not allow his people to settle down in a rut of mediocrity, but insisted that they persist and constantly move forward until they had secured their own long-awaited Promised Land. They moved forward restlessly but ever toward a divine destiny of greater good. What an inspiration his life, and all that it symbolizes in the journey of the soul, has meant to me in my own progressive growth toward a greater good!

I salute the courageous Joshua who dared to lead his

people through *so much* to claim their long-awaited Promised Land. I can identify with the pioneering spirit of Joshua, and as you use his fabulous success secrets described in these pages, I am sure you can, too!

HOW THEY PROSPERED IN THE PROMISED LAND

Yes, through meeting change nonresistantly, the Hebrews' dreams came true:

At last they had found a home in their very own rich Land of Canaan. After many centuries of city life, followed by forty years in a barren desert, and seven years spent in aggressively taking possession of Canaan, they were finally able to return to the simple life of their ancestors.

Remember that the word "Canaan" means "realm of substance." Gaining an understanding of the inner realm of substance as the foundation of all outer wealth is not an overnight process. Like Joshua and his followers, we gain that understanding degree by degree.

Now that they were in possession of that Land of Canaan, they were prosperous shepherds and farmers. Each man owned a piece of that rich Promised Land. Each family possessed its own dwelling place which seemed like a castle. They became emotionally and financially secure in their prosperous, new surroundings.

After having moved an elaborate portable tabernacle about in the wilderness for so many years, it must have given the Israelites a further sense of security to finally set up a great shrine at the city of Shiloh. There they worshipped in a tabernacle filled with priceless gold, silver and brass — in the splendid tradition set by Moses in the wilderness. To that richly adorned shrine, they joyously brought the abundant tithes of the Promised Land. These were graciously received by the priests, some of whom were adorned in bejeweled clothes similar to those earlier described by Moses as "garments for glory and beauty." (Exodus 28:2)

Although the priestly tribe of Levi was given none of the Promised Land, Joshua appointed forty-eight cities and towns in which they could live supported grandly by the generous tithes received from *all* of the Promised Land. Their faithful worship of God and their lavish tithe-giving at Shiloh would keep the Hebrews secure in their prosperity for many years to come. The word "Shiloh" appropriately meant "peace of mind, wholeness, security, abundant good."

What a contrast in their new life style to that formerly spent in Egypt where they had been forced to live as overworked outcasts in the slums. Joshua had taken those disorganized, frightened, runaway slaves and forged them into a nation of free men. Their dreams had come true:

"So Jehovah gave unto Israel all the land which he sware to give unto their fathers; and they possessed it, and dwelt therein. And Jehovah gave them rest round about, according to all that he sware unto their fathers . . . There failed not aught of any good thing which Jehovah had spoken unto the house of Israel; all came to pass."

(Joshua 21:43-45)

Yet the best was yet to be. This was the beginning of a national glory, the fame of which was to fill the whole earth! Theirs was a millionaire heritage. Acquiring the Promised

Land of Canaan—or gaining an understanding of the "realm of substance" as the key to all wealth—assured them of that wealth. They were destined to become one of the most affluent and influential groups of people the world has ever known.

Although Joshua had been born a slave in Egypt, he spent his last years as the revered leader of his people in that fabled land of abundance. Remember that the word "Joshua" means "Jehovah makes rich." After a careful, detailed distribution of the Promised Land to his followers, Joshua unselfishly waited to be the last to receive his own portion. At his request, he received the rich hill country of Ephraim where he built the city of Timnath-serah. (Joshua 19:49,50) This would indicate that he spent his last years amid total prosperity since the word "Ephraim" means "doubly fruitful," and the word "Timnath-serah" means "a multiplying portion." His eminence was universally acknowledged, and his death at 110 was deeply felt.

HOW YOU CAN PROSPER THROUGH CHANGE

You, too, can reap the vast benefits of the acceleration of change when you recognize change for what it is: expansion into a greater good. You can meet change through experiences of restlessness, dissatisfaction and even through apparent failure and loss by declaring that something good is coming from those changes. When you do so, like the Hebrews you will find your dreams coming true! Like the caterpillar that became a butterfly you, too, will know what Tennyson meant when he said:

"Men may rise on steppingstones of their dead selves to higher things."

To help you experience the prospering power of change, declare often:

"I welcome change and call it good. All things work together for good, even the changes in my life. To live and to grow is to change. If I hold fast I fail, but as I let go I grow. I willingly do the will of God in each situation. I accept my divine expansion now. I welcome the acceleration of change, and I benefit vastly from it now. I look upon every change as a new beginning so I am doubly prospered by it. Yes, as I meet life nonresistantly, my own life becomes fruitful, satisfying and productive of good. My 'cup runneth over.' I now enter my Promised Land where I belong."

SUMMARY

1. After Joshua took the Hebrews into their Promised Land, he spent seven years helping them take possession of it. Then he divided the property and gave each tribe its rightful portion.

2. The first assignment of land, the vineyard country of Hebron, went to Joshua's long-time friend and associate, Caleb. It was considered one of the most important and prosperous areas in the territory of Judah.

3. At the age of 85, Caleb was still strong and vigorous. He enjoyed his well-earned prosperity in the Promised Land.

4. Under Joshua's leadership, a portion of the Promised Land was set aside for the female descendants. Now they were given the right to inherit.

5. After establishing "divine order" among his followers in their new surroundings, Joshua then retired to the hill country of northern Palestine, where he serenely viewed the rich Promised Land that he had proudly won for his people.

6. When Joshua felt the change of death near, he called the Hebrews together and reminded them that God had been the source of their supply and enduring success. This same basic success secret was to lead them to phenomenal success in the years to come.

7. Joshua did not resist nor resent the change that was coming for him and his followers. He knew that change was a time of growth; that change was good and necessary, both for him and for the Hebrews.

8. The human nature of man is inclined to resist change, though the spiritual nature of man insists upon it. Letting go of the old is usually harder than taking hold of the new. To resist change is to stop your growth. A change indicates that "your growing is showing."

9. The soul demands change for its expansion. If the caterpillar could refuse to change, it would miss becoming a butterfly. Change cannot be by-passed. It can only be temporarily avoided. The soul of man goes through many changes in the course of a lifetime, if that person is growing, expanding and making progress.

10. After Joshua's death at 110, the Hebrews were ready to progress more on an individual basis, so they appointed judges to rule each of their twelve tribes. Although Joshua had been born a slave in Egypt, he spent his last years as the revered leader of the Hebrews amid total prosperity. His eminence was universally acknowledged.

In Conclusion . . .

THE DIVINE COMMISSION FOR ENTERING YOUR PROMISED LAND WHERE YOU BELONG

I trust that you have enjoyed this exciting story of Joshua's gradual rise out of limitation into abundance, of his ascent from slave to millionaire, of his great victories and vast accomplishments; and that you realize that all the blessings that came to Joshua can come to you, too!

Even though Joshua had resolved most of their problems as a group, when the Hebrews began to expand on an individual basis during the time of the Judges, there were new challenges to meet and new worlds to conquer.

It is all a part of the fascinating fabric of life. *New cycles of growth bring new lessons to be learned and new benefits to be gained.* But in the Land of Canaan, the Hebrews were evolving in their understanding of substance as the key to all wealth, and how to claim it individually and collectively. You can benefit vastly from what they learned as you use those same universal success secrets today.

In my future books in this continuing "Millionaires of the Bible" series, I look forward to sharing with you much more of their glorious destiny and how they attained it. Their success story can be your success story too!

Meanwhile, I invite you to meditate often upon the familiar divine commission that had been given Joshua in the wilderness, before he crossed over into the Promised Land — a commission which he fulfilled so well. *It is a divine commission for you, too, as you move forward out of limited wilderness experiences into your Promised Land of greater abundance where you belong:*

"Behold, Jehovah thy God hath set the land before thee; go up, take possession, as Jehovah the God of thy fathers hath spoken unto thee; fear not, neither be dismayed."

(Deuteronomy 1:21)

"Only be strong and very courageous, to observe to do according to all the law, which Moses my servant commanded thee; turn not from it to the right hand or to the left, that thou mayest have good success whithersoever thou goest.

"This book of the law shall not depart out of thy mouth, but thou shalt meditate thereon day and night, that thou mayest observe to do according to all that is written therein; *for then thou shalt make thy way prosperous, and then thou shalt have good success.*"

(Joshua 1:7,8)

SPECIAL NOTE:

You will enjoy studying the companion book to this one entitled *The Millionaire Moses, His Prosperity Secrets For You.*